A YEAR IN WAITING

A MEMOIR

Nicholas D. Butler

Third Edition
Printed in the United States of America

ISBN 979-8-234-03859-3
Library of Congress Control Number 1-8450911871

PROSAIC

Prosaic Publishing
Phoenix, Arizona

@prosaic.publishing

Cover design by @nickbutlerphd
No Artificial Intelligence was used in the composition of this manuscript

For my restaurant family;
and all those in waiting.

3

MENU

ACKNOWLEDGEMENTS

petit fours ○ gratitude ○ thanks

8

PROLOGUE

hors d'oeuvre ○ exposition ○ résumé

12

CHAPTER 1

GROWTH REQUIRES CHALLENGE

amuse-bouche ○ ordinary world ○ introduction

16

CHAPTER 2

CHALLENGE REQUIRES OPPORTUNITY

potage ○ call to adventure ○ backstory

26

CHAPTER 3

OPPORTUNITY REQUIRES VISION

oeuf ○ refusal of the call ○ context

30

CHAPTER 4
VISION REQUIRES EXPERIENCE

farineaux ○ crossing the threshold ○ immersion

34

CHAPTER 5
EXPERIENCE REQUIRES ALLEGIANCE

salades ○ tests and characters ○ genealogy

50

CHAPTER 6
ALLEGIANCE REQUIRES DEDICATION

poisson ○ the abyss ○ checklists

84

CHAPTER 7
DEDICATION REQUIRES PERFORMANCE

legumes ○ revelations ○ bravura

94

CHAPTER 8
PERFORMANCE REQUIRES COMMITMENT

entrée ○ refusal ○ disappointment

114

CHAPTER 9

COMMITMENT REQUIRES TRUST

roti ○ reward ○ relief

120

CHAPTER 10

TRUST REQUIRES HONESTY

releves ○ catharsis ○ judgment

128

CHAPTER 11

HONESTY REQUIRES COURAGE

sorbet ○ resurrection ○ conclusion

142

CHAPTER 12

COURAGE REQUIRES GROWTH

savoureux ○ the return home ○ reflections

146

EPILOGUE

entremets ○ a new hope ○ dénouement

170

RECOMMENDATIONS

l'addition ○ review ○ au revoir

172

ACKNOWLEDGEMENTS

This collection of memories is equal parts personal catharsis and professional homage to anyone actively pushing the boundaries of their abilities.

At the time of this publication, my year as a waiter had ended like being cut off at a bar: my career as an educator had been shaken, my marriage was on the rocks, and the shot of quarantine was a chaser too many. Life had overserved me a series of cocktails resulting in a hangover that took me months to recover from. During the Spring of 2020, I nursed my mental and emotional state in a tiny apartment that slowly began to feel like a hospital bed that I could only escape through the window that writing provided.

The original intention of this manuscript was to document my experience working in fine dining to develop an ethnographic academic journal article for publication on Food Communication that would hopefully turn into a larger project editing a textbook for students of the hospitality industry. Yet, as society considered how we might collectively reset during the period of COVID to move in a more positive direction, the writing process kept taking me to a state of personal reflection: Why did I become a teacher?

What kind of educator did I want to be? Why did I get married? Why did I become a waiter in the middle of my life? And what did I want to accomplish with my remaining time?

Meditating on these questions during an abrupt period of isolation during quarantine provided an invaluable opportunity to re-evaluate my perspective, so it's with immense gratitude that my inner circle of friends and family nurtured the direction of my writing toward a memoir dedicated to the millions of educators and service professionals struggling to find the words to motivate ourselves to continue to serve others with our remaining dignity. Specifically, I'd like to thank Kirt Shineman, Paul Morris, Doug Cunningham, Jess Dunn, Michelle Hill, Daphne Quinn, my mentor John Robert, as well as my editor, Aaron Hopkins-Johnson, for listening to what I had to say and offering their honest reactions to early drafts of this manuscript. Although the names of my colleagues at the restaurant where I had the fortune of working at for a short period have been changed to character roles out of respect for their anonymity, I hope they know how much their dedication to elevating the art of fine dining truly humbled and inspired me. Your life's work *matters*—especially to me.

Similarly, the personalities and establishments at the forefront of Arizona's food scene have a reserved table in my heart. Surviving in the desert is hard enough, but thriving requires a level of tenacity that the majority of the public fails to acknowledge. Hence, my writing this section! In turn, my profound admiration goes out to all of the nominees and recipients of national culinary awards from Arizona for their examples and contributions to our community. However, I never would've accepted my role in fine dining without the positive encouragement from my dearest friends in the industry who I will always admire: Chefs Joshua Reisner & Keenan Bosworth of Pig & Pickle, Todd Sawyer of Atlas Bistro, Chef Tammy Stanger of Cotton & Copper, tastemakers Bobby Lindeman and Dakine Beckman, Chefs George Murkowicz & Dara Sprinces Wong of Shift, Tyler Christensen of SoSoBa, Jordan Bartkowiak of Rewined, Jim Klever, Bill Brooks, and Celia Putty of Plazma, Jon Buford & Patrick Ware of Arizona Wilderness Brewing, and Dustin Hazer & Mike Conley of Helio Basin Brewing.

Regardless of where you live, I can guarantee that there are local residents who have dedicated themselves to advancing the way we cultivate, craft, and consider what we consume. My ultimate hope in publishing this memoir, beyond manufacturing a level of personal closure for the past year of my life, is to share a reverence for what leaders in hospitality do in our communities and encourage readers—far beyond this historical moment of existential crisis—to support their endeavors through our daily decisions when it comes to purchasing food and beverages. Together, I sincerely believe we can bring further humanity to the grinding pressures of the service industry and provide an example for workers of all professions toward a more sustainable future.

PROLOGUE

1 June 2018

Dear Members of the Hiring Committee,

This letter is to apply for posting #603745 as a Lecturer of Communication Studies at Northern Arizona University. My record as a professor and mentor at the collegiate level is ideally suited to provide experienced support for your vacancy teaching high demand lower-division courses with large enrollments. I earned my Ph.D. in Educational Technology with an emphasis in Applied Communication (2012) specializing in developing and evaluating online Public Speaking courses. As a doctoral student, I was recognized as a Fulbright finalist and my dissertation was published in *Voice and Speech Review*. I also have Masters degrees in Communication Studies (2012) as well as Film & Media Studies (2009).

In my most recent academic position, I created three new graduate courses and evaluated the curriculum of over a dozen classes for Arizona State University's Master of

Liberal Studies Program. On a 1-5 (Excellent-Poor) scale, my overall instructor rating was a 1.2 across 15 sections. Prior to moving to Arizona, I taught overseas for the University of Maryland's Global Campus on American military installations across Europe. During my time abroad, I instructed and supervised the development of hybrid Communication and Humanities courses for hundreds of active duty soldiers working towards their Associates degrees. This unique position provided an excellent opportunity to teach in a multicultural environment as I successfully integrated hybrid learning design practices into overseas curriculum. While at UMGC, my classes doubled in enrollment due to notably high evaluations and word-of-mouth support from students who rated the courses I taught and designed a 4.7 on a 5.0 (Poor-Outstanding) scale across 16 sections—culminating in a Teaching Recognition Award for the 2015-16 academic year.

As a graduate student, I managed two grant-funded projects while serving as a Faculty Associate teaching undergraduate courses. I developed a large-scale (167) student distance-learning course and managed four teaching assistants at ASU's West campus for an Organizational Communication grant project. The course was recognized by Quality Matters as a model for course development in the Blackboard Learning Management System and is still in use. Additionally, I developed a series of instructional videos for candidates in the Mary Lou Fulton Teachers College and managed the collection of student-teacher interviews on a grant from the Arizona Higher Learning Commission.

From 2008-14, I gained experience with strategic planning as the head coach of ASU's nationally recognized competitive speech program. During this period, I planned and managed dozens of speech & debate tournaments for high school and college students across the country. I also managed the team's speech competition budget, coordinated travel plans for students, and regularly taught workshops on Public Speaking. In 2014, I hosted the National Collegiate Speech Tournament for over a thousand participants—an undertaking that required two years of devoted budgetary and logistical planning as well as supervising a staff of dozens in order to successfully execute.

While I no longer coach on a regular basis, I've maintained external partnerships in the speech and debate community since 2008 and currently serve as the President of the International Forensics Association, which hosts an annual speech and debate tournament in alternating countries every year. Likewise, my record of service as an active committee member and conference planner for the National Communication Association for over a decade demonstrates my sense of professional duty.

In addition to the 10 years of experience I have in higher education as a teacher, coach, manager, and supervisor, I also served as an officer in the military after I graduated from the U.S. Air Force Academy. During my service, I supervised dozens of soldiers as the Officer-In-Charge of the Honor Guard for the region of Southern California, managed deployment readiness and scheduling as an Executive Officer, and oversaw an annual budget of over a million dollars for service support operations as a Flight Chief at Edwards Air Force Base.

In summary, I meet all of the desired qualifications listed in the job description of an ideal Lecturer in Communication Studies: a doctoral degree in the field, a wealth of experience teaching Communication courses, a significant record of instructional innovation, service, and professional development, and a commitment to promoting diversity in our community through service as well as civic engagement. Should you have any questions, I invite you to contact me directly or consult my references. I'm available to be present for an interview if selected as a candidate and look forward to the prospect of joining your department in the Fall semester. Thank you for your consideration and taking the time to review my application materials.

Sincerely,
Nicholas D. Butler, Ph.D.

CHAPTER 1
GROWTH REQUIRES CHALLENGE

With a family name like Butler it was only a matter of time before I became embroiled in the restaurant business. Some of my earliest childhood memories are of being in the kitchen peeling potatoes with my mother, in the garden harvesting tomatoes with my grandfather, and tagging along with my father hunting and fishing across the Great Lakes. If you trace my family lineage back far enough, our name comes from Boutelliers who would tend to the bottle collections of British and French royalty, so it's fascinating to consider how conditioned my epigenetics are predisposed to serve others. It's something I've thought a lot about over the course of the past year while scrubbing tables until they're spotless, mopping the floor until it shines, setting tables to precisely mirror one another, polishing silverware and glassware until it looks like new, folding napkins like origami, cleaning bathrooms to military standards, building table arrangements like a florist, endlessly rearranging chairs and tables for optimal spacing, steeling my nerves to transport priceless dishes from the kitchen in choreographed ballet service so as not to disrupt the culinary paintings they display, and gracefully navigating the minefield of guest expectations and team standards to create one of the most memorable dining experiences in the world.

If intelligence is truly measured by one's mastery of specialized knowledge in a given field, my friend (who will henceforth be referred to as our Chef) is a true visionary and world-class technician in the kitchen. Prior to opening his first restaurant over 15 years ago, he started his career after graduating from culinary school by working in Patrick O'Connell's Michelin-starred *The Inn at Little Washington* where he met his Spouse—a lifelong industry professional in her own right. Together, they spent five years working at Thomas Keller's world-renowned *The French Laundry* where our Chef slaved away on the kitchen's hot line with future culinary superstar Grant Achatz. While Chef Achatz went on to found *Alinea* in Chicago to extraordinary herald, our Chef stayed in Napa and ultimately became the Chef de Cuisine at *The French Laundry*, responsible for executing the menu by working side-by-side with Chef Keller.

From personal experience dining at all three of these celebrated institutions, my honest opinion would be that, like Chef Achatz, our Chef has surpassed his mentors. He has emerged as a proven leader among the current generation of culinary innovators produced by such celebrity chefs as O'Connell and Keller over the past several decades. As a result, our Chef's dishes are more challenging in terms of ingredients, ambitious in terms of presentation, and down-right delicious in terms of combining complementary flavor profiles—but I guarantee you've never heard of him outside Arizona.

Why? In his words, he refuses to "play the game" by appearing on television and volunteering his skills at events for free. Most people would consider his demeanor "Old School," but the truth is more complicated. The best in any field know *better* when they see it. And when it comes to cooking, being the best means being in the kitchen full-time without distraction. It takes the stamina of a boxer. It means when you do get a day off, you spend it eating at other restaurants, reading cookbooks, and sketching out new ideas to try out on your next shift. It's all-consuming.

When I first met our Chef and their Spouse, they were in the midst of opening their first restaurant and simultaneously operating small catering engagements to make ends meet. They moved from Napa to be closer to family in the Southwest, initially planning to leave the service industry after years of back-breaking labor that routinely demanded "100-hour work weeks." But they couldn't resist the opportunity to finally have their own establishment where they would be able to run the kitchen and business according to their own standards. Beyond our Chef's imposing height and cropped beard, my initial impression was that he was supremely confident in his craft and socially engaging with a razor-sharp wit. During the day he always wore weathered t-shirts, chinos, and rubber non-slip shoes, but during service he always suited up in a crisp classic button-up chef's coat. His Spouse was equally charming and knowledgeable, but clearly preferred to operate behind the scenes. Her hair style regularly changed and she often opted for a cotton tunic in the afternoon before zipping into a little black dress for service. Through our first conversation, my husband and I found a shared interest with them in contemporary art that eventually grew into a relationship where my husband's art gallery began supplying works on consignment to the restaurant when it officially opened in the Spring of 2005.

The original concept for their restaurant was to allow guests to select the number of courses they would like (for example, four to six courses) from different sections of the menu (such as appetizers, main courses, or desserts). The restaurant was located in a strip-mall on the outer reaches of Phoenix, so diners tended either to be from the neighborhood or self-proclaimed "foodies" who made the pilgrimage for the experience. The space was intimate, with approximately 30 seats, but the atmosphere set by the contemporary décor and relaxed waitstaff was designed to be disarming. The floorplan included a waiting area surrounded by a glass-enclosed wine collection, a small host station guarded the dining room, and a cozy bar with six seats peered through a tiny window into the kitchen that functioned as a pass for orders that were ready. Humorously, our Chef was so tall that he needed to bend down in order to speak to anyone through the pass, so it was rare to see anything but flashes of his torso dashing back-and-forth in the kitchen. On one occasion, I can recall being escorted by his Spouse to the kitchen and stunned by its approximation to a child's bedroom in size. They started building a new home together, so it was little surprise once they finally received national recognition in their first year that their household began to grow in the form of more restaurants in the way that young couples bring children into the world.

10 years after its inception, our Chef's brand flourished to successful operations at four different locations. However, instead of continuing to expand, as any rational business model would encourage, our Chef came to the realization that they weren't happy managing multiple restaurants that were growing beyond his exacting standards of quality control. He knew that if the small franchise continued to expand then guest's experiences would ultimately suffer, and such a result was simply out of the question. His motive had admirably evolved from a financial bottom-line into a vision of elevating the cultural conception of dining in the entire geographic region. He wanted all of his children under one roof.

In turn, our Chef began to consolidate his four restaurants into a central location by selling the other three successful operations and changing the design of the remaining restaurant to model a traditional dinner party at their home: beginning with a cocktail on the terrace, touring the restaurant that was formerly a residence, transitioning into the bar area for several small courses, and finally being escorted into the living/dining room where guests are seated as if they're audience members faced with a view of the restaurant's stage: an open kitchen. The response was overwhelmingly positive to the dinner party concept and quickly grew to become the most exclusive restaurant in the Southwest both in terms of limited seating (20 guests per night) and extravagant cost (a pre-purchased $200 ticket plus 22% gratuity and sales tax all before beverages).

However, the cost was even more daunting for our Chef. As they revealed to me in personal conversations, "The restaurant needed to at least sell tickets for 17 guests an evening just to break even." Failure to meet this goal meant arterial bleeding from the restaurant's revenue stream and threatened to close the public "home" they had built. Essentially, any profits from tickets and beverages went toward paying our Chef's mortgage (for their residence just one street across from the restaurant) or renovations to the business. Creating the ultimate dining experience for our guests represented the culmination of his life's work and compromising his vision for making it even greater every service wasn't an option. So, when I was approached to join the restaurant's staff, I was understandably overwhelmed by all of the unknowns. Why me? What would my role be? Why not select someone with more experience?

Our Chef called me in for a meeting in their private dining room one afternoon and explained that he knew I was frustrated with my current academic role, especially commuting, and was actively looking for my next job opportunity. He cited that I was "more passionate" about dining than nearly anyone else they knew with a "dining resumé" that served as proof of my dedication. As a Professor of Communication I possessed a unique perspective for helping improve the restaurant. He wanted someone he trusted and didn't want to go through the process and risk of hiring an unknown commodity. He assured me that I would be able to split my time between teaching and covering services, and his expectation was simply that I learn as much as conceivable as fast as possible.

Our Chef took a moment to crunch the numbers on a calculator and showed me a sum. He was willing to pay me $180 per service (to later be negotiated based on my performance) *without tips*—which were pooled and collected by the house. He explained that I would be shadowing his General Manager (the GM) and primarily working with three other waitstaff: a Bartender, an Expeditor, and a Busser. His answers to my initial questions seemed reasonable enough as someone with no professional experience, but as a social scientist I knew that testing our Chef's assumptions would require direct experience. I also needed my husband's blessing, so our Chef gave me a few days to decide.

Since losing my job at Arizona State University, my marriage painfully became more of a business partnership than a relationship I could confide in and trust for refuge. In addition to owning an art gallery, my husband had taught for over 30 years and was in a comfortable position to retire before I fell on hard times. As a result, the situation fueled dozens of arguments about how "I needed to provide more income" so he could retire as planned from teaching and spend time at the gallery at their leisure. The pressure to find work was intense, and the longer I went without long-term employment the more demanding he became without actually providing any assistance other than paying for our mortgage. There was actually a point when he told me he would no longer be proof-reading the cover letters for job applications I was submitting on a daily basis because it was "too stressful" for him.

To make matters worse, his expectation was that I *only* apply for jobs close to home. Ironically, accepting the offer to commute to Flagstaff to teach actually embittered them more than the sacrifices I made to hold on to gainful employment as an educator, so falling short of hitting the career lottery within a few miles of our home was the only solution to our problems he could see for us. Admittedly, it was the only solution I could see at the time, too. I wanted to provide what he *wanted*, but I also needed to find a line of work that could provide what I *needed*. Working at the restaurant presented a twist that neither of us had anticipated. $180 per shift wasn't much. It was less than half of what I made as a professor for a fraction of the time, but it was close to home and in a new field that we only knew about from one side of the table—but deeply admired as diners.

Aside from the pay, my husband's petty concern about working at the restaurant was getting "too close" to the GM, who he suspected had designs on me, but I could sense that his unspoken concern was the perception of *lowering myself* to becoming a waiter after decades of education to earn my doctorate. Was joining the service industry really my calling? I didn't know, but wanted to try. After all, the job was close to home and meant extra income while I was still teaching, so my husband tepidly gave his consent like a parent giving permission for their child to go on a field trip. We agreed that I should give fine dining a shot until the end of the academic year before reevaluating it's sustainability and weighing any other potential job opportunities that might present themselves in the next six months.

The following afternoon, I accepted our Chef's offer on face and began my year as a "Visiting Professor" at the restaurant. I desperately wanted to make it all work—finding a balance of professional worth, happiness in my marriage, and the gratification of helping my friends—so the endeavor began to symbolize the only path toward salvation. I was at a crossroads with one foot in higher education and the other in a new world: the service industry.

CHAPTER 2
CHALLENGE REQUIRES OPPORTUNITY

The people who struggle in business are those who trade their labor for a wage and daily consider quitting. The people who thrive in business are those who profit from the trade and never consider changing. Make no mistake, higher education is just as much of a business as running a restaurant.

I never imagined that my life as a teacher could become more difficult than after the cover letter in the prologue got me hired at a second-tier college in Flagstaff.

One moment I was grinning on a glorious April day at the thought that I had finally found the right role for me as a college professor, and the next I was overwhelmed with tears trying to figure out how my career at one of the largest universities in the country could be completely derailed by a phone call. My supervisor was mystified, explaining that he had just been pulled aside by our Dean after a meeting about an "informal complaint" from the Athletic Department—not coincidentally after I failed two starting

Division I football players. He notified me that my contract would no longer be renewed as scheduled. That was it. No rationale. No farewell cake in the lounge. No opportunity to defend myself. Just a phone call and a wall of silence from the administration. Due to the trauma the experience caused, I still have trouble speaking on the phone, but there are some calls that you simply can't refuse.

I spent the entire Summer begging for adjunct teaching gigs to no avail until my phone rang two weeks before the academic year began. The call was from an area code (928) near a college where I had applied to teach, so I took the chance and answered. It turned out Northern Arizona University needed an emergency hire for a Lecturer position in their Communication Department. The call was brief, and the answer was an emphatic, *Yes!* The following day there was a phone interview with a panel, then another with the program director, and by the end of the week I was preparing to teach four new classes on a campus two hours away from my home.

Orientation was like a fever dream that I couldn't wake up from. Beyond the usual piles of paperwork and unnecessarily endless meetings, it took days to get the keys to my shared 10" x 20" office space with five other Lecturers. My desk was void of a chair and outfitted with a decade-old Dell computer without a keyboard. So much for working from my office. Moreover, the curriculum provided to me consisted of weekly quiz banks and generic slides, so I needed to build the vast majority of the curriculum for all of my sections from scratch—a task that usually takes the majority of a summer. The situation was like waking up in a maze and hearing the footsteps of a minotaur drawing closer. There was nowhere that I could afford to rent (or hide in the metaphor) so I was staying in a roadside motel. My schedule required me to wake up every Monday at 5am to drive to my 8am class with 85 students (and no teaching assistance), teach my other three classes scheduled for Monday/Wednesday and Tuesday/Thursday, and then drive home on Thursday evenings.

To make matters even more complicated, before the first week was even over, I was approached to teach a fifth class on Screenwriting as an overload since the assigned instructor was still awaiting their Visa. I was the newest professor in the department, and eager to prove that I deserved to be hired on a longer-term contract, so I accepted. At least I could write about what I was going through, I thought: lecturing to five classes with four preparations, having two emotional breakdowns three weeks after being hired, and holding on to the singular hope that something good would one day come of this nightmare. I didn't realize it at the time, but the classic storytelling textbook for the Screenwriting course I was teaching, Joseph Campbell's "The Hero with a Thousand Faces" (1949), was ominously aligning with the challenges I was facing in reality.

Four months later, the stress of the role eventually subsided after I was able to finish developing the curriculum for my courses, get to know my students, find a few allies in the department, and use my benefits to see a psychiatrist for the overwhelming anxiety and depression I was experiencing. I felt like a computer that had run out of bandwidth.

Thankfully, my evaluations were enthusiastically high, the staff at the hotel had started treating me like a member of their family, and the commute had given me an opportunity to catch up on some reading by listening to audio books. My schedule for the Spring was lining up to only require me to be on campus Mondays and Wednesdays, with simply one new class to update that I had taught dozens of times before. The coming semester appeared to offer a welcome period of stability and much needed rest. However, I never could have anticipated receiving a call during the last week of classes from a close friend with an even more unexpected challenge in mind: help him run one of the best restaurants in the world.

CHAPTER 3
OPPORTUNITY REQUIRES VISION

To provide some context as to why I might accept an opportunity to help our Chef in the middle of an already exhausting academic year, the following letter was penned to my friends and family as a holiday message explaining how I was coping with my professional role in the world:

The past twelve months have been some of the worst of my life. Perhaps I'm going through a midlife crisis. Perhaps I haven't been challenged enough. Perhaps we're living through a shameful period in history. Perhaps this is a multiple-choice exam and all of the above apply.

It all started with writing to the Athletic Director of my former university about the poor performance of two of their starting football players who lied, cheated, and eventually failed one of my graduate courses—a film survey section they were enrolled in as an "easy" class to sidestep NCAA regulations. My contract was rescinded two weeks later. My benefits were gone by the end of the month, and I spent the summer with insomnia desperately applying for jobs.

After months of trying to keep my head above water, I finally received what seemed to be a life preserver thrown to me by my current university, but accepting the position to continue teaching essentially meant starting my career over from scratch at a new institution as an emergency hire. Commuting at 5am every Monday to teach over 200 students, sharing an office with five people in quarters that would normally accommodate two, and returning on Thursday afternoons with no semblance of security in my future has felt like being lost at sea.

This year taught me a lot about the current state of higher learning in our country and even more about myself. I, and arguably we, have trusted the wrong leaders in our lives and it's time to stop being exploited. When I lost my job, I received lots of sympathy, but no one stood up for me professionally—much less financially.

Accepting a position at another university has only been a thankless endeavor that's benefited another institution at my expense, so I'm left mulling a unique vision of the future that my dear friends recently shared with me: stop doing what makes other people richer and start doing what makes me happier. I should distance myself from tyrants and their theifdoms to stay closer to home and enrich my community. I should stop stressing myself to the point of fracture to explain material to students who could readily watch a presentation online if they were truly interested. And I should stop associating with supervisors who aren't invested in my growth as well as institutions who turn a blind eye to abuse.

Surviving this year has left a scar that I will always be marked by, but it certainly won't define me. Perhaps it's time to take a step in a different direction in 2019 instead of staying in the same place I feel like I've stood in for the last ten years. I'm done waiting.

To see me during this moment was to see me at my most manic and vulnerable. Our Chef saw the exhaustion in my body one day as I was delivering a keg of beer that my father and I had brewed for the restaurant. He heard the frustration in my voice, and sensed the unrest in my heart. He recognized that I needed an opportunity to grow in a new way. His restaurant had just lost their sommelier and he needed someone to manage their beverage program as well as consult on continuing to refine their dining experience. Of course, I had dined at their restaurant many times as a friend and someone who celebrates the crafting of beverages and cuisine, but I had never worked in a restaurant before.

Beyond being a home brewer who helped supply the restaurant with its own exclusive taps, he knew I was a Professor of Communication with a background in Public Speaking and Performance. He knew I was a capable actor fascinated by the concept of fine dining and gastronomy as culinary theatre. And he most certainly knew I had no idea about what it takes to cut it in a world-class restaurant. Anyone else in my position would have emphatically replied, "No, thank you," but I knew that I was reaching a breaking point in my professional life as an educator, struggling to find work closer to home, and desperately needed someone I could trust to help guide me forward. So, as much as my brittle body and sputtering mind told me to politely decline, my heart told me I couldn't possibly refuse such a once-in-a-lifetime call to adventure.

CHAPTER 4
VISION REQUIRES EXPERIENCE

Our Chef had a vision for my role in the restaurant, but I had no frame of reference for what it would take to simply make it through a day's shift—much less succeed as a service professional at an elite establishment. Our Chef regularly cited the day his restaurant opened as if it were a birthday and I likewise recall my first shift on 19 December 2018.

Arrival, per the GM's instructions, was expected by 12:45 and everyone parked next door in order to leave ample space for delivery vans, product representatives, as well as guests. Protocol dictated that we always enter the restaurant through the backdoor and arrive ready to work—generally in a t-shirt, slacks, and sneakers—along with a suit bag to hang in the office with our "uniform" for service. Once inside, the first order of business was to greet the kitchen staff to alert them of our arrival and immediately begin cleaning the dining room. Keeping the wooden floor in proper condition necessitated sweeping, vacuuming, and mopping on a daily basis. In order to cover every inch of the space, chairs and tables were shifted to one side of the room and then the other. Depending on the number of guests and the size of their parties, tables would be exchanged for the proper size and number from a storage shed in the back of the restaurant. For example, a couple needed to be seated at a "deuce" and a party of six needed a larger "six-top". The tabletops were made of reclaimed wood and weighed approximately 50 pounds. Each tabletop needed to be separated from its base (another 50 pounds) in order to be moved in two parts. Using a dolly and working as a team were highly encouraged, but everyone could undoubtedly haul a tabletop or base with their bare hands. Lifting and moving items in the restaurant like an ant was a considerable part of the job, so it quickly became clear to me why everyone on the staff could hoist more than their bodyweight.

Once the dining room was clean and the right number of tables and chairs were staged, the next task was to consult a seating diagram designed by the Spouse before we arrived and printed specifically for the evening's service. The daily diagrams detailed who, where, and why everyone would sit in predetermined places during segments of service, so setting the dining room, bar, and patio required exacting attention to detail. Failure to conform to the seating diagram or make unapproved changes meant suffering the wrath of the Spouse. Moreover, the restaurant's expectation of precisely setting items on the tables symmetrically with one-inch spacing took pain-staking focus.

As the GM instructed me, napkins were centered between a guest's chair and placed one inch from the edge of the table, bread and butter dishes were centered on the napkin's left at one inch distance, silverware was centered on the right of the napkin on a metal device (akin to a chopstick rest) at one inch distance, water glasses were centered above the silverware at one inch distance, wine glasses were set one inch and 45-degrees away from the upper left of the water glasses, and candles were to be refueled and set either in the center of the table for a six-top or six inches away from the opposite end of the table from couples at a deuce. In terms of attention to detail, the GM represented the most extreme reverence for place setting protocols and the Busser's contributions would routinely be readjusted. Training my eyes to see all place settings the way the GM did was of particular importance, so I began using the exact length on a pen (and later a mark on my thumb) to double-check place settings until my eyes could notice something offset from 20 feet across the room like a hunter sighting movement in the forest.

After the dining room was set, we applied the same principles to the bar area as well as the patio. Napkins, plates, silverware, glasses, candles, flowers, repeat. I was responsible for double-checking everything—centered with one-inch distance between all items—and if a spot appeared on a glass or piece of silver it was my responsibility to polish it out.

As our Chef emphasized, his "obsessive" qualities would really kick in if he noticed anything "off" in the dining room like a detective, so it was imperative not to distract him if we wanted to avoid comments like, "Tighten up the fucking dining room or I'll find someone who can!" After all, surface appearances were our guest's first impressions of the restaurant, so there was no room for error. All tables needed to be leveled and balanced using small plastic "wobbles," all chairs needed to be dusted and wiped down, and every surface would be scrutinized for the persistent appearance of debris throughout the day. If anyone walked in for a delivery and sat down, it meant erasing any signs of their momentary presence.

In no other aspect of the restaurant was this expectation emphasized more than the bathrooms—an endless chore that the GM was all too relieved to pass on to me. "People can be such animals," he disclosed. "Look at this! That fucking delivery guy just took a shit like a shotgun blast and didn't even clean up after himself!" In turn, it was our duty to scrub away their extra deliveries. On a daily basis, bathrooms were to be sanitized and polished to hospital standards. Furniture was moved out, medical gloves were donned, and every surface was sprayed with a generic cleaning agent including bleach. Precisely rolled linen hand towels were stocked by the sinks and the edges of toilet paper were folded into aesthetically pleasing triangles. Once the bathrooms were mopped, the understanding was that they would only be used in the event of an emergency rather than make us clean them all over again—which I rapidly learned was the expectation during service. Any time the bathroom was used it needed to be cleaned, so you can imagine the looks one would receive if they went anywhere near the toilets after they were mopped. The anxiety surrounding maintaining pristine surfaces led to such an ingrained policy of avoidance that I can't recall using the restaurant's bathroom during my first month.

Once the bathrooms were spotless, my next assignment was to learn how to prepare the bar for service by shadowing the Bartender. Foremost, the Bartender taught me that every item in the bar has a designated "home". Space was tight in the 6'x12' area, so optimizing the placement of everything in order to fill a drink order in less than a minute was imperative. Items in the reach-in coolers were organized by wine varietal along with a section for sodas and beer that all needed to be restocked daily. Cocktail shakers, stirring spoons, straws of three varieties (especially eco-friendly paper ones), teas from around the globe, espresso, citrus, and over 30 types of bar glasses on a five-tier shelf all had their own homes. Need to use a muddler? No problem—just make sure it finds its way home. Failure to do so spelled failure during service by wasting precious moments scouring the restaurant for a muddler with the fervor of searching for a missing child in a supermarket who had wandered away.

Similarly, all cocktails were the product of exacting recipes that I was expected to commit to memory and become familiar enough to make to order during service. If I needed a reference point for an obscure request, there was a recipe book behind the espresso machine, but the vast majority of orders thankfully came from our limited menu of six cocktails or ten bottles of wine by the glass. In the absence of the Sommelier, the GM or the Spouse would handle table-side bottle service for the time being, but learning the proper way to present, open, sample, decant, and pour wine into the exact center of the glass without dribbling around the brim like I had been doing it my entire life was a heaping portion of responsibility that was readily piled on to my brimming plate.

Moreover, any remaining time after accomplishing our daily checklist was conscripted by the kitchen to help prepare our shared "family meal" before service as well as plate dinner courses that could be staged on shelves in the walk-in cooler. Helping in the kitchen was intimidating for most members of the front of the house, but lending a hand chopping onions, juicing lemons, making a salad, roasting eggplants, layering flavors in a soup, or whatever the kitchen needed that didn't require molecular gastronomy was well within my abilities as a domestic cook. Like working up front, spending time in the kitchen meant learning techniques and protocols at rapid fire speed that took weeks, if not months, of adjusting to the hypoxic altitude in the restaurant.

There was an optimal way of doing any task and that was the only acceptable way. You think you know how to cut citrus into wedges? Sure, there are plenty of ways to cut oranges for youth soccer players to enjoy at halftime—but the most optimal way is to roll the citrus on the counter to ensure you get as much juice as possible, lop the top and bottom portions off, cut the remainder in half, remove the center pith along with seeds, then slice the halves into equal quarters. Our Chef showed me how to do this in less than 10 seconds and the expectation was that I commit those 10 seconds to memory and cut citrus that way for the rest of my life. That was the pace and intensity of working, and in my case helping, in the kitchen. If you need to walk to fetch an ingredient, you need to drive in a traffic pattern on the right side of the kitchen and do it at top gear. Malaise in the kitchen was like falling asleep at the wheel and meant you might physically get run over by a semi truck. Any trip to the pantry or walk-in cooler meant you better ramp up to haul your cargo and stay in your lane as you merged into traffic on the kitchen's Autobahn.

Thankfully, there was a moment in every shift when everyone would take a short 15-minute break to sit down and have something nourishing to eat during our family meal that always featured a protein, starch, vegetable, salad, and fruit. Knowing that shift meals were often an afterthought of leftovers in Styrofoam in most restaurants or consisted of a gut-pack combo meal in a paper bag—if they even existed—our Chef's kindest act was ensuring that we always had some sustenance served on ceramic dishes with silverware for the effect of feeling at home. Most weeks were themed, such as Russian or Puerto Rican cuisine, so the kitchen staff would force themselves to learn new techniques and test them out on the staff. Sometimes the most substantial portions of meals humbly consisted of eggs and tomato sauce, but there were also extravagant days when we indulged in jumbo shrimp with Thai curry. We never knew what we would have to eat, but family meals quickly grew to become my favorite part of the day and something I took gratification in helping prepare when I had time to help in the kitchen.

The small window of time between our family meal and our daily meeting was generally reserved for getting dressed for service and sneaking a moment to tend to correspondence on our phones before stashing them in the office for the rest of the evening. Meetings started promptly at 4:30 and were led by our Chef. We started with notes from the previous service, such as "Why was there a fucking candle out at the end of service? Candles should always be lit!" and comments from "call-backs" our Chef made to guests that morning. Notes—however nitpicky—were always critical, but constructively served the purpose of continuing to refine our discipline and improve our guest's experience.

Once our Chef's notes and guest comments were reviewed, the floor was open for anyone to add their comments, but this rarely happened. Input from the staff was generally limited to the kitchen expressing their annoyance by an area not being thoroughly wiped down or an item not finding its designated home. During my first weeks, I tried to provide some positive reinforcement, but those sentiments were quickly discounted and outright discouraged as "wasting time." This was a restaurant—not a classroom.

After comments were vented, the second half of the meeting was dedicated to reviewing the details of the menu and any guest allergies for the evening's service. To the testament of the kitchen's dedication, any allergies (or more commonly preferences) were accommodated by providing a substitution. For example, the culinary team would bake entirely different loaves of bread for anyone who was gluten free and faddish keto diets received alterations to virtually every course out of 20. Bringing the wrong dish to a guest with a restriction was one of the worst mistakes we could make during service, so every course was reviewed, allergies were highlighted on all checklists, and seats were precisely numbered.

Once reviewed, we rehearsed the menu aloud by going around the table and having everyone randomly describe different courses and having our Chef correct our phrasing down to a refined script we committed to memory. The amount of information to process was staggering. I have been in plays, competed in speech and debate, given lectures to halls of hundreds of people and taught for a decade—but nothing in my career compares to digesting an evening's required stagecraft and elocution of delivery for service. After 30 years in service, the GM was the only person who could (and was allowed to) perform the role of hosting, serving, and describing all the courses. My primary task as his understudy was to learn his role in less than a month.

Mercifully, my responsibilities for the first week during service were to, "Stay out of the way, study, and help as needed." Unless someone specifically asked me a question, I was to avoid interacting with guests until I rehearsed the proper answers in front of the GM and demonstrated memorizing the weekly menu in front of everyone during meetings. Until then, I could pour water, help carry dishes, and ensure the bathroom stayed spotless by cleaning it after every use. It may not seem like much, but people drink water in the Southwest like they've just returned from being lost in the desert for days. By our Chef's decree, no water glass should ever be less than half full, so the simple concept of keeping water glasses brimming quickly became a headache.

Additionally, every dish needed to be held in a proper way by using the area where your palm meets your thumb in order not to leave evidence of a fingerprint on the plate. Guests *always* needed to be served from the left. If a guest had items in front of them, we would shift the dish we were carrying to the other hand, clear space, place the dishes in synchronized fashion, and then shift to the guest's right to clear any finished items. "Serve from the left! Clear from the right!" It sounds easy, but when guests do things like lean on the table or stack their dishes on the left, it quickly becomes frustrating to do things according to protocol when it would be much easier to clear from the left.

Moreover, every table had unwritten numbers assigned to each chair that we needed to memorize every shift, so walking dishes from the kitchen meant you were assigned to a particular guest. For example, "You've got position 3 at Table 2." The system is simple in theory, but if you counted wrong it potentially meant a guest might receive an item they were allergic to and you would be walked to the back of the kitchen outside the earshot of diners and our Chef would lay into you like a college football coach. "What the fuck are you doing trying to fucking kill someone out there?! Pull your head out of your fucking ass! If you ever fucking make a mistake like that again—you're fucking gone!" And it would undoubtedly be brought up at our meeting the following day. The shaming would continue, and the GM would be assigned to figure out a protocol on top of the existing protocol to ensure the mistake would theoretically never happen again.

Meanwhile, guests constantly use the bathroom. Anytime someone stood up, the nearest person was responsible for making their way to the table, pushing in the empty chair, intricately folding their napkin, and tidying the space by wiping any crumbs or clearing any empty dishes. By the time the guest returned to their magically transformed place setting, the nearest person on our staff would pull out their chair to help seat them, and I made my way to the bathroom to clean any signs of their existence like The Wolf from *Pulp Fiction* being called in. It was as if they had committed a crime we were helping cover up. Guilty of not standing close enough to the urinal? Don't worry—we've got a specially trained team we'll send in. Can't remember if you left your fingerprints near the homicide? No worries—we'll be your alibi. It's rare that a guest leaves the bathroom as they found it, so maintaining their cleanliness during service when water was waiting to be poured and dishes were languishing in the kitchen was a necessity. As we were often told by the Spouse, "Be like a shark that's constantly moving and hungry to bite into the next task!"

By the end of my first service, being corrected for serving from the wrong side by the Expeditor, rebuked by the Spouse for marking the wrong type of wine glass, chastised for neglecting water glasses by the Busser, and being reminded of details like restocking a hand towel after a guest used the bathroom by the GM, had amounted to receiving a term paper with more red ink than text. There were literally *hundreds* of corrections I was expected to make, and they needed to be made by the next day. That, and we still needed to clean up! While the evening was winding down, we were assigned to stand by in case a guest might want a night cap, needed their water topped off, or had a coat checked. By design, we were always several steps ahead of anticipating guest needs, so there was always someone ready to make a drink, fill a glass, fetch a coat, and open the door to deliver an earnest farewell. Putting the guests first meant putting off any ideas of cleaning until we saw the taillights of the last vehicle leaving the parking lot and heard the phrase, "All clear!"

Once the signal was given, we raised the house lights, snuffed the candles, and collected the flowers. All tables were given an additional wipe down before moving them to the north side of the dining room along with the chairs, so we could immediately start our checklist the following day. Breaking down the bar meant melting the ice, washing barware by hand, cleaning the mats, and flipping all the chairs onto the counter. Breaking down the patio entailed gathering all of the cushions, moving all the metal furniture into groupings that were locked outside, and bringing the wooden furniture inside. When I started, it took most of my strength to move one of the metal chairs at a time, but several months into service I could carry one in each hand with ease like emerging from a training montage in *Rocky*.

Awaiting us like unwanted packages inside, glass racks were always stacked by a large table in the bar where we gathered around in a knitting circle and polished glasses for at least an hour, but typically closer to two. Everyone had their own technique for polishing glasses: the Busser used a wet shammy in one hand and a dry one in the other, the Bartender used a single shammy that was half wet, the Expeditor used two shammies that were both wet in one corner and dry in the rest; and, to the amusement of everyone, I brought in a white polishing glove that I wore on one hand and used a half wet shammy in the other. "Oh, shit!" the Expeditor would say, "The glove's coming out." And everyone came to know that all I wanted to do was focus on polishing glasses as fast as I possibly could so we could go home. The Bartender and the Expeditor loved to talk shit and take their time, but at the restaurant polishing was the bane of my existence and my superpower as "The Glove" was quickly embraced as a method of shaving time off of our shift—which regularly lasted until 1 or 2 am.

By the time we finished polishing all the glassware and returning everything to its proper home on the shelves, I was always exhausted. We were always exhausted. During the first week, my feet were riddled with blisters and ached from the distance covered over the course of the day—a mistake I immediately corrected with heavier socks and orthopedic dress shoes with thick rubber soles. I was no longer a stylish diner in colorful socks and chic loafers. I had literally stepped into a completely different side of the dining experience: one that threatened to physically wear my body to the bone, overwhelm my mind with boundless amounts of information, and test the very limits of my spirit. I made a commitment to work in the restaurant for a year, and it was going to last longer than I could ever imagine.

48

A YEAR IN WAITING

information, and test the very limits of my spirit. I made a commitment to work in the restaurant for a year, and it was going to last longer than I could ever imagine.

CHAPTER 5
EXPERIENCE REQUIRES ALLEGIANCE

During my hiring process, one of the items that our Chef emphatically stressed was how he no longer wanted to hire anyone after me. The restaurant's staff, by intention, would continue to whittle down like the cast of a horror movie until only the most allegiant remained. When I joined, the Sommelier stayed on for an extra week to help provide some continuity, but my actual on-the-job training was predominantly left to a 21-year-old undergraduate (the Bartender) who had worked at the restaurant in one form or another since he was 16. As a college professor, this was a humbling turning of the tables, but the truth was that our young Bartender was incredibly knowledgeable (for anyone's age), thoughtful in the way he nervously walked me through the myriad protocols, and genuinely invested in our success as a team. How he knew so much about alcohol only months into his legal tenure was a question I felt better left unanswered. After all, I wasn't the one doing the teaching when it came to business at the restaurant.

The Bartender

As it turned out, not only was my training supervisor the age of my students, he was actively pursuing a degree at my former university. Hence, the only person who seemed more mystified by my presence than myself was the only person still enrolled in school and conditioned to harbor some mild reverence for my academic standing. Thankfully, the novelty wore off quickly as we began wading through our daily checklist of items to accomplish (detailed in Chapter 6). The Bartender made it clear that it was expected that we would arrive 15 minutes early every day and immediately greet everyone in the kitchen. This seemingly wholesome act initially endeared me to the emphasis of the staff according to our Chef functioning like a "family"—however, the gesture also served as a practical barometer of how you were functioning at the start of a shift: Were you upbeat? Were you drunk? Were you on something? Greeting the kitchen staff was a way of gauging our utility that day. Regardless of the way you actually felt, it was critical to start the day on a positive note. No one was better at this than the Bartender who struck me as the type of student who "participated" a lot during class, but might not be doing the amount of work outside the classroom that his activity level while being observed seemed to imply.

Like so many students I encountered over the past decade, he was pursuing a degree in Business.

Appearances were important to him—especially at the restaurant. He always had product in his hair and wore sportswear during the day before completely changing for service. His smile and genuine excitement were ideal for hospitality, but his age still carried an air of anxiety when interacting with guests. Moreover, his parents played an active, if not overbearing, role in his budding career, and the restaurant was regularly cited during our training sessions as a point of disagreement between them. He wanted to continue learning about fine dining and maybe become a restaurateur, but that wasn't practical enough for his parents, who were regular diners at the early version of the restaurant. Like me, he was trying to keep a foot in academia as well as in the service industry and I could tell that it was taking its toll. I saw a lot of myself in the Bartender, and he was genuinely excited to have me join the team. We spent the majority of my first few weeks working side by side, so his seasoned insights gave me the first glimpse of what my impending future held.

The skill I most admired in the Bartender was his ability to make virtually anything that you could dream of to drink. Grasshopper? No problem. Over-the-top flaming Tiki drink? Sure thing. Half-half no whip mochaccino with crumbled candy cane on the rim and a side of Amaro? With our pleasure. Nothing phased the bartender. Challenges from persnickety guests actually invigorated him. Of his many professional feats of strength, two hours before service one evening a table of 12 Latter Day Saints guests requested a non-alcoholic beverage pairing for their meal. They were willing to pay $50 per guest. Could we do it? Without hesitation, the bartender immediately started crafting a menu and gathering ingredients. In terms of presentation, the end result looked exactly like the entire table was drinking alcohol all evening (for example, a cola and tea infusion served with a hand-carved ice cube looked like an Old Fashioned). Eight different non-alcoholic drinks to pair with dinner for 12 guests that required nearly all of our bar glasses. The execution was flawless and everyone at the table agreed with me. Guests from other tables actually asked what they were drinking and wanted to order a round of the same until they found out they were non-alcoholic. That night I marveled at how gifted and seasoned our Bartender was and how much I would have to learn to even come close to his wunderkind level of expertise.

The Bartender taught me how to use a three-compartment sink to wash, rinse, and sanitize dishes; inventory and stock beverages with their labels faced consistently centered like a high-end grocery store; make cold-brew coffee using a three-foot high Taiwanese apparatus; divert the espresso machine's steam to also make tea and simple syrup; master the recipes and techniques necessary for making all the house cocktails on the menu; and, most importantly, how to gracefully leave one's position in the restaurant once you eventually found a worthy, if not woefully unenlightened, replacement for your role in the family. As much as I saw the Bartender excel, I also witnessed him understandably crack under the pressure of our Chef's expectations on several occasions, including one in which he needed to sit down in the bar in a fetal position to steady himself because he dropped two dishes in a row at the same table.

Carrying miniature sliders on delicate ceramic dishes across an entire restaurant in one hand and placing them in front of guests without making a sound in a precise position was something no one could do if they thought about it too much, and the Bartender had clearly thought about it a lot over his formative years. So it was understandable that by the time Valentine's Day arrived, the Bartender, more than likely at the behest of his parents, finally mustered the courage to break away from his long-term relationship with the restaurant and give his two-week notice so he could focus on his studies.

From his perspective, I had been trained "enough" and he had clearly been waiting for the opportunity for a while. It was time to leave the nest and I was grateful for his guidance. In turn, true to our Chef's prognostication, instead of hiring another bartender the GM announced that I was taking over bartending duties for the foreseeable future. In addition, of course, to my main priority of learning the GM's responsibilities now that I had completed my initial training.

The GM

Familial descriptions of responsibilities in a restaurant are often used to describe the roles one plays in the family business. In ours, the GM played the role of our Chef's responsible older brother—someone who was born a decade before, learned from his mistakes, and offered a more level-headed perspective when his younger sibling got ahead of himself. While our Chef served as the expert on all things culinary, the GM functioned as our sage of hospitality. Working in restaurants his entire adult life had turned his body into the build of a distance runner and whittled his eyes to sharp points that hid behind his librarian glasses. He reigned in his curly hair by keeping it tapered, which came to serve as a metaphor for me of their spirit being bridled by the discipline they deeply required from their work. He always wore suit pants, dress shoes, and a button-up shirt in the afternoon before changing into bright (typically contrasting) colors for service. Greeting and interacting with guests, properly setting tables and arranging seats, serving and clearing dishes according to etiquette, and hawkishly supervising our discipline were his primary responsibilities during service. However, the GM's daily checklist of tasks went well beyond the scope of the amount of preparations and "side work" the Bartender had trained me to accomplish.

Like our Chef, the GM had moved to the Southwest in order to be closer to his family, so the sibling analogy holds true. Moreover, he previously worked at the iconic Chef Charlie Trotter's legendary restaurant in Chicago for over twenty years. Edmund Lawler's book *Lessons in Service from Charlie Trotter*, which I read for guidance during my early weeks at the restaurant, draws several sections directly from our GM's impressive contributions. Growing from his experience at Trotter's was a badge of honor he subtly reminded of us by exclusively using the wine key he had earned as a Floor Captain there. Trotter was notorious for verbally and economically abusing his employees, so the GM's exacting standards and expectations for the front of the house readily equaled those of our kitchen. Perfection was his objective, and our Chef often remarked to guests that "without the GM the restaurant wouldn't continue." The restaurant was their shared labor of love as veterans of the service industry; and, as they both freely expressed, it was the "final stop" on their professional journeys. Hence, training to perform the GM's role came with a daunting amount of professional responsibility and familial duty.

Keeping up with the GM was like shadowing a hummingbird. The sheer volume of tasks to accomplish multiplied by the expectation that they all be accomplished perfectly was enough to make the average person start hyperventilating. As a learner, listening to the GM during training was like the adage of drinking from a fire hose. The number of protocols concerning when to do a task, how it should be accomplished, and why it needed to be done precisely in said manner were innumerable. During the time I trained with the GM, I would often describe the experience to friends and family as learning 100 new things a day. He was conditioned to operate in top gear like the BMW coupe he drove, and I was accustomed to driving the speed limit on cruise control, so it took a while to catch up.

On the first day that I shadowed the GM, we both arrived 15 minutes early, greeted the kitchen, and immediately went to the office to listen to phone messages. He gave me the number to call for voicemail, shared the password to the computer, and showed me his method of recording notes from the messages into a logbook that would serve as the next checklist after we listened to the 18 messages ranging from a person simply stating their first name and leaving a phone number to three-minute descriptions of each guest who was attending and their acute dining preferences without leaving a return number to call. You learn a lot about guests by the way they conduct themselves before they ever arrive.

To complicate matters, the phone was horribly antiquated. You could barely hear anything (especially when the vacuum was running) unless you turned on the speaker option and cranked the volume to its maximum. Hence, when guests would rapidly say their name or phone numbers it would require listening to the message multiple times, which turned out to be the case for virtually every other message. I tried to suggest modernizing the restaurant's system by using digital services like OpenTable or Tock, but the tone implied by facilitating a personal interaction with guests was central to the GM's sense of professionalism.

Once the messages were recorded, "callbacks" were conducted in order to answer questions and secure reservations. Often, the requested date was unavailable, so quelling frustrations and rapidly finding acceptable alternatives was of paramount concern. Phone etiquette was to follow a rigorous script that seemed lifted from *Downton Abbey*, but with a tone of "excitement" by a guest's interest in dining with us. Answering the messages—not to mention answering the phone throughout the day—quickly became one of the most emotionally exhausting tasks the GM taught me; hence the rationale for why messages were attempted to be accomplished first, followed by email, and ultimately postal deliveries. Yes, *postal deliveries*. Have you ever dined at a restaurant where you've felt compelled to write a "thank you" letter the following day? Our restaurant received them at least once a week, and (not to be outdone) we would always reply with our own letter of thanks on official restaurant stationery.

After tending to the day's correspondence, the GM would leave the office to review the table and seating arrangements in the dining room, bar, and patio. If a table looked slightly misaligned, he would adjust it. If a chair was placed askew, he would correct it. If there was dust on the base of a table, he would clean it. If a table wobbled at all, he would level it. All while muttering under his breath about why the other members of the front of house staff couldn't get it right *the first time*. Once all perceived mistakes were rectified by the GM, the go-ahead was given to begin setting the napkins, silver, plates, glassware, candles and flowers—all undoubtedly destined to be rearranged once the GM returned from his next task.

Outside the "floor," or the main area where guests dine, the GM and the Spouse were also responsible for maintaining the room where wine was cellared and updating its inventory as a function of his added role of helping me cover the responsibilities of the former Sommelier. The restaurant's collection of approximately 700 bottles was stored in five temperature-controlled coolers in a room that hosted our daily staff meal and on rare occasions doubled as a private dining room. Shipments arrived daily, and the menu's beverage pairings necessitated alternating inventory space on a weekly basis, so the GM tracked everything on a printed spreadsheet with a numeric system (for example, wine in the third cooler and twelve racks down was annotated 312) that was updated in pen. As it turned out, he and the Spouse hadn't had a chance to conduct a complete inventory in months, so my next responsibility was to complete an entire update while the GM whisked away to ensure the table settings were perfected. Thankfully, annotating spreadsheets and performing basic arithmetic were already parts of my skill set, so I took some satisfaction in being able to meet his expectations on this particular assignment.

Once the inventory was complete and the GM returned, we advanced to the patio to inspect the exterior of the restaurant. All the light bulbs were to be checked and replaced as needed, gas in the heaters and fireplace was to be tested, windows and surfaces were to be polished, and plants were expected to be trimmed and maintained. Even details such as a leaf turning yellow or pine needles (that were constantly falling throughout the day) appearing on the deck of the patio were never to be overlooked. When doing yard work at home, the phrases, "Why are there yellow leaves on this plant?" and "Sweep this shit off the patio!" still echo in my mind. These were the details, as the GM often cited, that separated the "good" restaurants from the "great". Being good was never enough; and, as I came to understand over the time we worked together, the burden of *greatness* was a standard that weighed heavily on the GM. In the restaurant business, once you experienced excellence through a dish or via service there was no substitute. It's an obsession in the world of fine dining.

In no other aspect of the GM's duties was this philosophy more ingrained than attention to detail once the daily checklist was complete and dinner service began. Guest placement was pre-assigned and rehearsed not only by table number, but by their alternating seats in three different phases of the meal. Pronunciation of guest's names, their titles, special occasions, dining preferences, and any allergies were all rehearsed. The way certain seats were served, the manner in which particular dishes needed to be carried, the exact order and precise placement of every course were all pre-arranged. In coordination with our Chef, descriptions of dishes and details about their sourcing as well as preparation were scripted and refined by the GM.

Everything from clean-cut grooming and confident demeanor to proper pathways to walk in and prescribed responses to guest questions were all devised by the GM, so to see him personify his expectations of the staff on a daily basis was to see someone at the height of their abilities. To see the GM walk through the dining room with the agility of a cat, spot guest needs like a sniper, communicate nonverbally to us how to address them, all while clearing an entire table's doll-sized ceramic dishes in one hand, answering a question about an obscure detail relative to the current course's sourcing, and picking up two empty Burgundy glasses without the guests even noticing was truly a sight to behold. I thought I had seen amazing service in my dining experiences, but to be on the other side of the table with the GM on your team was to know the answer to any question—and the answer was always, "Yes".

In turn, when the GM's father passed away only a month into my training, there was never a hesitation on my part to accept his responsibilities in the short term. The opportunity to work with the GM and study his craft first-hand was one of the main reasons I decided to work in the restaurant. Once I started to understand what he personally sacrificed in order to commit to a life in service to diners was truly inspiring. Covering his duties during the period he was absent (the only time in years that he had taken leave) was both an honor as well as a baptism by fire. Operating at full speed during the day, being a leader on the floor during service, and covering closing duties into the wee hours of the morning processing checks, printing checklists, and going through elaborate lock-up protocols was something few people on the planet could manage. I took immense pride in never bothering the GM during his absence, but it took every ounce of my willpower. Keeping up with the demands of the role that our Chef and their Spouse had grown to assume would be covered felt like crawling through glass, but by the grace of the restaurant gods I made it to the other side of that scene from *Die Hard* having proven myself as a survivor.

The Spouse

If there was anyone who doubted my commitment to the restaurant after my brief performance as the GM's stand-in, it was the Spouse—who was eminently more capable and qualified than myself. Like our Chef and the GM, she had spent her career in high-end restaurants, but I suspected her continued presence during service grew out of a commitment to her marriage rather than an insatiable calling. After 15 years helping run the restaurant, she originally told me as a friend that her plan was to start distancing herself from working during service so she could focus on what she truly enjoyed: tending their garden at home, arranging flowers, filling gift bags with fruit from their trees, and printing menus in the morning before the front of the house staff would arrive. The more distant she was from the restaurant's exacting protocols and interacting with guests, the better she felt. Not that the rest of us didn't feel the exact same way, but it was far more complicated for the Spouse having to submit to our Chef's demands during very audible arguments and then act like a bubbly host during dinner service.

To make matters worse, I quickly became the symbol of anchoring the Spouse to working on the floor since it would take a significant amount of time to train me as an acceptable substitute for the Sommelier. By the direction of our Chef, the combination of the Spouse and the GM (who technically had not completed Sommelier training themselves) were to handle bottle service for the foreseeable future. They were directly responsible for teaching me volumes of knowledge as well as how to imitate decades of experience until they could return to their preferred responsibilities.

To the GM's credit, he developed several helpful training sessions on wine varietals and pouring etiquette that were hosted in the brief minutes following staff meetings. However, the Spouse didn't see the point. In my opinion, she knew our Chef's professional standards better than anyone and that learning it all on the fly was far too much for even the brightest of students to master in such a short period. She understandably seemed to feel trapped performing an exhausting role in a Broadway production for an undetermined amount of time.

Moreover, separating the personal from the professional proved difficult for us both. Rather than making the effort to work with me before service, she immediately grew irritated with the single two-minute lesson she taught me the entire year on the "proper" way to open a bottle of wine and shifted to a more punitive method of snarling at me if I made the slightest of mistakes that were unbeknownst to me until she bit down. "If I need your help, I'll ask for it!" is a line that echoes in my mind as well as the oft recited "Why the fuck are you walking dishes before wine's down?!" The barbed hostility began during service, but after the first few weeks it bled into whenever our paths crossed during the day when she would demonstrably greet everyone in the restaurant with the exception of me.

As longtime friends who bonded over being introverts and having sarcastic senses of humor, it was a tough time for us both having to navigate how to maintain the highest of standards with a quickly lowering morale. The day's mood during prep rested on the temperamental nature of our Chef, but the harmony of an evening was critically signaled by the Spouse's attitude when she arrived moments before service began. We never knew what to expect, so always braced for the worst, and there were several nights when she walked out in the middle of service leaving us scrambling to recover. An apology or explanation the following day was never provided, and we knew wiser than to make the situation worse by pulling the scab off a perceived wound.

When I started working at the restaurant, the Spouse used to play "Saturday" by the Bay City Rollers over the speaker system to get everyone in an upbeat mood, but after a few months the tradition gradually faded away. She wasn't happy and we all knew it. As much as I tried to make amends and learn as much as I could about wine, she had made her mind up about my role in the restaurant: at best, I was going to be a temporary foster-child in the restaurant's family.

The Expeditor

The person I grew the closest to was responsible for expediting food during service and generally encouraging us to "hurry up" throughout the day. Think of a celebrity chef barking at everyone to get orders right and move as quickly as possible—without the threat of a bite—and that's the Expeditor. He started as a dishwasher two years prior to my start spending months in the dish pit making $8 a day while going through rehab at a group home. For nearly a year, he ran the cleaning crew until he finally got a chance to wear a second-hand suit and work in the front of the house helping clear tables.

He had spent time in prison and the experience had literally left its mark on his body in the form of tattoos of allegiance. He dealt a lot of drugs at an early age and done even more, especially when it came to intravenous narcotics. So, try to imagine the combined expression of earnest disappointment and restrained rage on his face when I showed up for my first day of service and he immediately realized I was going to be jumping him in the restaurant's hierarchy. "Who's this fuckin' guy?" the Expeditor said to the GM. We were nearly the same build, age, and appearance (minus the tattoos), so guests would regularly ask if we were brothers. We had clearly made life choices that were diametrically opposed but had somehow ended up in the same place.

On a surface level, the Expeditor was my death metal doppelgänger, but over the course of our year together, we became as close to adopted family members as anyone else in the restaurant's family. When he and his wife moved into their first place, I brought them a couch from our spare room. When I learned his back had been killing him from sleeping on a futon after our long shifts, I rented a truck and brought them our extra bed. When he finally got to a point with his ex when he could have his children for brief visits, we all went to the movies. When he finally completed his years of probation, we celebrated his sobriety and freedom like a newborn's birth. Watching the Expeditor slowly rebuild his life to reach a point of independence normally associated with a student going away to college was equal parts heart-breaking and inspiring.

His life had been difficult—far more difficult—than I could ever understand. One of his parents had introduced him to narcotics at an early age, his intelligence was appropriated to help sell drugs, and his addiction had ravaged every relationship he had ever valued. Dodging warrants for his arrest and spending time in prison where he was forced to racially affiliate himself in order to survive hadn't left him many opportunities to establish roots in a community and commit to sobriety, so seeing him embrace the opportunity that working in the restaurant offered was truly profound.

Having served in the military and coached college speech students, I thought I had heard the boundaries of crude language and first amendment rights, but the Expeditor wove a tapestry of obscenity on a daily basis that would make the father from *A Christmas Story* blush. In the environment of the restaurant (as I've been told most kitchens operate) shit-talking is like a second language; or, in the case of the Expeditor, a superpower. Within moments of his arrival, it would be loudly announced whether he had sex that morning and how he performed, what his impressions were of last night's guests and who they amusingly looked like in popular media, as well as the meaning of the last song he heard on the way to work—invariably a metal song he would continue to sing pieces of throughout the day until we were all echoing the lyrics. Without the Expeditor, the restaurant was a monastic space in terms of noise. Music and Talk Radio were outlawed by the GM as "distractions" from our work, so the Expeditor's colorful language and stories provided some much-needed comic relief to ease the tension associated with executing the items on our daily checklist with exacting precision.

Beyond making sure items on the checklist were steadily accomplished during the afternoon and dishes were rapidly moving out of the kitchen during service, the Expeditor's duties generally centered on helping whoever needed an extra set of hands. Anything from leveling tables and folding napkins in the front of the house to cleaning the fryer and chopping onions in the kitchen, the Expeditor was the Swiss Army knife in our Chef's back pocket. As the adage goes, idle hands do the devil's work, so it made sense that the Expeditor found stability in the pace and intensity of fine dining. He had never dined in a restaurant like ours, but that wasn't the aspect that appealed to him—the work was his salvation.

The Expeditor taught me how to accomplish all the odd jobs that he was tasked to figure out during his tenure: how to pick the locks to the office and bathrooms when they jammed, how to reach the uppermost shelves in the dining room from the top of a ladder with an extended feather duster, how to use a vacuum sealer to preserve leftovers from the kitchen, where to set the sprinklers in the garden to achieve maximum efficiency, the delicate nuances of when to ask our Chef for leniency or a favor, and the hundreds of protocols during service devised by the GM that were unique to the restaurant. Service was often like storming the beaches of Normandy in *Saving Private Ryan*, so having someone like the Expeditor on your side kept everyone moving toward the machine gun nests with reassurance.

When it became clear that my time at the restaurant wouldn't be long-term, the Expeditor took the news the hardest. He marveled at how fast I could learn complex tasks, memorize extravagantly detailed menus, and interact confidently with guests. "You'd be awesome at prison," he once told me. "You're so smart you could run a store from your cell and get a flat screen. No one would mess with you." I took his words as a compliment. The longer we worked together the more the Expeditor understood our Chef's reasoning for hiring me as a floor manager, but he couldn't relate to having options beyond the solitary opportunity in their life that the restaurant symbolized. Even though he didn't have the passion of our Chef or the lifelong commitment of our GM, his loyalty was committed to serving the restaurant without question.

Beyond the earshot of our supervisors, however, the Expeditor admitted that he wanted to quit on a regular basis. Every time our Chef needled him with remarks like "Get your head out of your ass!" or the GM ridiculed his grammar whenever he said phrases like, "I seen it," a flash of fury would spark in the Expeditor's eyes. "It would be so easy to quit and fucking rob this place," the Expeditor remarked to me on several occasions. But he always calmed himself with the known outcome if he did. In his words, "It'd be *all bad*," but as much as he sometimes loathed his duties as an indentured servant to the restaurant, he knew he had finally found a home.

The Busser

The person everyone knew the least about was the Busser. It was possible he was actually older than the GM, but he never revealed his age. I can't recall a day when he didn't wear Jordan sneakers and a name brand t-shirt to work like we were at basketball practice. He preferred the baggy look even when it came to suits, which were typically pinstriped like a mafioso. He kept his hair short and could never seem to decide whether to keep his mustache or not. The Busser spoke English, but tended to avoid conversations out of general disinterest and a habit of guarding his mystique like a character in a telenovela.

He was from outside Mexico City in Huauchinango and shared with me that he had crossed the border three times. He didn't say how, and I didn't think it was my place to ask. He worked the same hours I did, received a printed paycheck, paid taxes, and rented a humble apartment converted from a garage near the restaurant where I dropped him off after work. That was enough for me. On the weekends he played soccer in a rec league and watched football in his favorite sports bar. With no spouse or children, he stuck to himself and led a fairly quiet life outside the restaurant.

According to our Chef, the Busser had apparently come with the restaurant as the seller's lone stipulation that he would have to make sure there was a job for him. Left with little choice, our Chef accepted the deal. In turn, that meant everyone in the front of the house, with the exception of the GM, had never worked in a fine dining restaurant before. In one respect, this worked economically for our Chef, but from a perspective of quality control there was an immense amount of training to be done. For example, the Busser had no perception of why it was so important to have everything on the table align symmetrically with an inch of space between all items. After all, "There's a fork, right?" Wrong.

Our Chef was constantly on the Busser's case for making the most minor of infractions such as not fully closing a swinging bar door on the way to the dish pit because he was carrying a tray loaded with hundreds of dollars in glassware. "How many fucking times do I have to bring this up at meetings? Close the fucking doors behind you!" The Busser had heard this on a weekly basis for nearly four years, so you can imagine that he developed a fairly thick skin when it came to our Chef's barbs, but it was quite the opposite. Every night when I drove the Busser home (a role I inherited from the Sommelier), he lamented how, "It's never enough. Chef's always wanting everything to be perfect, but there's too much to do. I'm marking all the tables. I'm pouring all the water. I'm doing hot towels. I'm clearing all the dishes. This shit is too much!"

In order to make up for his lack of polish and attention to detail, the Busser was relegated to performing the majority of the tasks that the GM didn't have time to accomplish and the Expeditor preferred not to do. The Busser would usually start the day helping us set up the dining room, but as soon as there was a pause, he began cleaning the exterior of the restaurant by blowing pine needles off the roof and patio, hosing bird droppings off the patio and parking lot, washing the dozens of windows from both sides, and then moving all the metal patio furniture into place. If there was an opportunity to work alone, he relished it.

Once I noticed his routine, I tried to lend him a hand in order to get to know the Busser a little better. "You want to help me fold napkins?" He was bowled over by my interest in learning what he was doing and trying to help. "No one's ever helped me fold napkins in four years. Here you go, amigo!" Each part of the restaurant, and even some courses, was assigned special linen with exacting folds that the Busser was responsible for accomplishing. An average of 24 guests per night times four different napkins, plus rolling hand towels for the bathroom as well as hot towels for guests at the beginning of service, added up to about 200 napkins each service. The linen came in stacks of 20 from the cleaner wrapped in plastic. The Busser would take five stacks, push me five more, and I tried to match his pace. We folded a lot of napkins. Usually in silence, but occasionally we bantered about our Chef's mood that day, the guests we had the night before, and the number of beverage pairings that were purchased for service that evening.

When it came to beverage pairings, four meant we might finish early, but that was rare. The average was normally half the number of guests, and the Busser was an expert at doing the math of how many glasses we needed to polish after service: 12 guests times eight pairings plus 24 guests times three rounds of water glasses and any additional beverage orders is about 175 glasses. Glasses were normally washed by the dish pit in racks of 4x4 or 5x5 before we polished them at the end of service, so the Busser would tell us how many racks we would likely have that evening. "Ah shit, homie. We're gonna have 10 racks tonight. We won't be done until 12:45. You'll see."

10 racks meant our shift would go at least past 12 hours. More racks meant more time donated to the restaurant. We got paid per shift, not by the hour, so beverage pairings and the racks they created became our natural enemy in the ecosystem of the restaurant. It may seem easy enough in theory to quickly dry a glass and set it on a shelf like you probably do at home, but the Busser had been chastised far too many times not to take the job seriously. Polishing glassware at our restaurant meant that every glass needed to look like new before it was placed on a tray and escorted back to its assigned shelf. If a glass was chipped in any way, it was discarded. If a glass had lipstick still left on it, it was washed by hand in the bar and redone. If a glass couldn't be held to the light and have zero trace of hard water spots from Phoenix water, it was polished again. We polished a lot of glasses. Usually in silence, until the Expeditor would join us and banter about the nights' service would kick into high gear. "Yo, Chef was pissed tonight. There was only one note: Close the fucking bar doors!"

It was as if the entire service was a complete failure if our Chef noticed the tiniest of infractions when it came to our discipline, and the years had taken their toll on the Busser. "Fucking, Chef. It's never enough. Why doesn't he notice how I clean everything outside? I wash all the windows. I fold all the napkins. I mark all the tables. I pour all the water. I clear all the tables. It's too much!" Unlike the Expeditor, the Busser hadn't found a home in the restaurant—he lost it in a trade—and it appeared there was no way out of the deal. He was stuck, and the longer I spent in the restaurant the more I began to feel the same way. We became hermanos.

The Kitchen

Traditionally, there's a clear division of labor and allegiance in restaurants depending on whether you work in the front of the house (dining room) or back of the house (kitchen). While our Chef was particularly adept at interacting with guests and happy to describe some of the courses himself, he was the unquestionable leader of Escoffier's "Brigade de Cuisine" (1903) responsible for anything related to food products, storage, preparation, and presentation. In turn, the GM was the natural leader of the front of the house, or "Maître d'Hôtel," responsible for everything from accounting and correspondence to maintaining the landscaping and ensuring the air conditioning ran properly. There was a literal threshold where the wooden floorboards of the dining room met the ceramic tiles of the kitchen and crossing it meant you were venturing into potentially hostile territory.

People in kitchens are among the hardest working members of society in terms of the length of time they spend physically working without breaks, mental focus needed to execute painstakingly detailed techniques, and emotional stability required to endure the constant verbal hazing.

Polished appearance, presentation skills, and basic interpersonal abilities aren't generally their strong suit, so those qualities were associated with what our Chef frequently referred to as the "front of the house strut". When I started, the kitchen staff included our Chef (the Executive), his Chef de Cuisine (Chief), a Sous Chef (Deputy), a Commis (Junior Cook), and a former dishwasher who became the Garçon de Cuisine (Assistant).

Whenever anyone from the front of the house went into the kitchen to help, they gravitated toward whoever treated them with an ounce of respect because the norm for kitchen staff was to constantly assert their role in the hierarchy in condescending fashion. Having known our Chef the longest, I usually asked if he needed any help first, but he would routinely send me to assist the Chief or Deputy who were always "behind" in their duties. Running behind to our Chef meant not accomplishing a task as fast as humanly possible, so failure to do so during the hundreds of tasks to execute in the kitchen meant that you were technically running behind by a matter of seconds or minutes. "Are you STILL doing that?" was a common dig from the kitchen staff when it seemed to them like a task was taking too long.

In turn, such pressure made asking kitchen staff the simplest of questions seem like an extreme nuisance to them at best and at worst the cause of mental breakdown. You know the way people stop walking in order to respond to a text message? That's what it's like asking someone in the kitchen who's in the middle of a task. Losing concentration meant losing time and the clock was always ticking. Kitchen staff were expected to time themselves to learn how long it took them to perform tasks, such as mincing a shallot or breaking down a pineapple. They could then multiply that number for the amount of produce as well as continue to try and beat their own times. There was always a way to do something faster, but the expectation was that you still used an optimal technique. Perfection requires repetition. When it came to peeling, paring, and chopping to create symmetrically perfect cubes for guests to consume the kitchen staff were capable of magical sleight of hand, but if you asked them where the flour was stored their mouth would gape as you could see the gears in their mind grinding to a halt before they could muster a vague direction of "In the back!"

Being in the kitchen was always intense, but not without purpose. Execution at the highest level requires extreme discipline, so being a part of the hierarchy in the kitchen necessitates submitting to anyone more experienced; especially our Chef. There was a reason his name was on the restaurant. He submitted years of his life to some of the most recognized Chefs in history and successfully ran his own restaurants for 15 years. Challenging his authority was never an option. The kitchen, as the term Brigade de Cuisine implied, was our Chef's small Army that was trained to operate like a Special Forces unit executing a dinner service. "Execute! Execute! Execute!" was a common phrase in the kitchen appropriated from the military. Perform your responsibilities as if lives were on the line in battle!

Few people can thrive in such an environment, so it was with little surprise that less than two months into my time with the restaurant that the Deputy was let go for turning to substance abuse as a method of managing the pressure and the Commis moved on to a less demanding role at another location before her hair started to grey in her 20's. A career in the kitchen isn't for most people. It can grind the hardest of personalities into dust, but the few who endure gradually emerge as diamonds in the rough. To listen to our Chef recount working for months on two broken ankles, scalding his feet with boiling water that sat in his sneakers while he finished the shift without medical attention, and noticing the scars from countless cuts and burns he had endured was more than a reminder of his mental and physical toughness. It was a testament to his discipline as a journeyman in the kitchen. There was *nothing* he hadn't accomplished or was willing to do in the kitchen, and that was the level of commitment he demanded from everyone around him. There was no other place he could possibly be in the world than in the back of the house refining his craft on a daily basis.

The Butler

If you haven't figured it out by now, I'm not the most stable of personalities—not to mention narrators—so it only seems fair to paint a similar portrait of myself from the perspective of my colleagues in the restaurant.

The Butler always arrived too early. It became obnoxious. I couldn't figure out if he was trying to make us look bad or was always hopped up on caffeine. You could tell he was in the military by the way he kept his hair short like it was a regulation. He always showed up in New Balance running shoes, suit pants, and an ironed white undershirt. At the start of the day he was usually like some chipper character from *Sesame Street* radiating positivity, but would quickly snap into playing the role of a cynical detective from *The Wire* as soon as things went sideways. They say that Mr. Rogers was a sniper in the Marines. I don't believe that, but for the Butler that didn't seem like it was out of the realm of possibilities. There was the network television version of him that guests saw during primetime and the explicit premium channel version that we were watching after hours. I couldn't discern whether it was from his background in the military or he needed some serious medication, but the man never had any chill.

As our Chef would say, he's "one of the nicest people in the world"—as a guest maybe—but he can be a brooding bastard when something sets him off. Whether it's a discussion about the placement of a table or an argument about who played the best James Bond (which was obviously Roger Moore), the Butler always has an opinion on the subject. He physiologically can't seem to keep his mouth shut when it comes to controversy. Most of the time I actually agree with him, but it's the *way* he digs in and won't give up that's exhausting to be around. Honestly, my butt cheeks have never clenched tighter than when I've heard him talk back to our Chef. It's like the man is riding into battle by himself and the rest of us are watching through binoculars from the safety of a nearby hill knowing that he won't survive the climactic scenes from *Braveheart.*

And when the Spouse arrives? They're like the most passive aggressive couple I've seen since high school. I don't know what the deal is between them, but they should text each other and break up so everything in the front of the house can go back to normal. The Butler knew more than any of us about beer and could make a helluva cocktail, but he's got a lot to learn about wine. Watching him try to open a bottle the proper way is like a child needing help to open a jar of pickles. I figured it would be easy for a guy who seems to memorize things so quickly to learn the process, but I guess everyone has their limits.

I remember the first time the Butler came in for service. He was only supposed to keep the bathrooms clean and maybe help us walk dishes to larger tables. By the end of the night, he was walking dishes on every course, making drinks, and polishing glassware like a champ. I can't knock the man's hustle. There was never a service when he was in the weeds. Did I see him mouth off to Chef and have to go in the office for words? Yes. Did I see him unload on our Chef de Cuisine like a nuclear bomb at one of our daily meetings? *Oh, yes.* Did he come through whenever we needed him? Most definitely.

To his credit, the Butler had a way with words. Words that I had never heard before, but sounded pretty. Describing dishes, especially during meetings with Chef, is one of the most stressful parts of service, but he made it seem so effortless. We would fidget with our hands, rock back and forth, and avoid eye contact with our Chef like kids in a classroom. Meanwhile, the Butler's sitting there like he's teaching a class. When we found out he was a professor, it all made sense—all brains and no common sense. He had to question everything instead of shutting up and getting the job done.

And notes during meetings? It's like he couldn't stop himself from suggesting ideas that we all preferred he keep to himself—especially this whole concept of giving guests a tour. It was hard enough moving guests through three sections of the restaurant throughout the evening. Now we have to give everyone a tour with dishes planted along the way like Easter eggs? If we were characters in *Clue*, I wish I could've murdered the Butler in the study with a wrench for that one.

Having him in the front of the house made us stronger and more confident, but it also tested our patience. He was the only person who ever seemed to get leave to go to places like Berlin or New York "on business" leaving us struggling to find a substitute, but at least he always brought back menus for the kitchen and new ties for us. I have to say that the man's suit game was on point, but don't tell him that or it'll go to his head.

Most guests loved him, but there were a handful of people who found him condescending, so there were a number of nights when we had to wave him off certain tables so the GM could diffuse any tension. I don't think it was ever his intention to come across like a snob or anything, he just couldn't keep his temper in check when guests would get demanding or down-right disrespectful. It got better as the months went by, and I can remember him saying he had started taking medication to stabilize his mood, but there was something deeply engraved in his temperament that wasn't sustainable in service. He was like a brother when it came to giving us everything he had on a nightly basis, but we all questioned how long he could last.

○ ○ ○

Together, we all served as extensions of our Chef's mind and body. His philosophy and vision became our mission. The Chief, Junior Cook, and Assistant were learning how to extend the reach of our Chef's impervious hands—hands that I saw reach into boiling water without hesitation, carry scalding pans across the kitchen oblivious to their temperature, and refuse to be cut by the sharpest of blades. Squinting through glasses, the GM was focusing on how to see our Chef's vision of reaching perfection in the unforeseeable future. The Expeditor was always listening for sounds of dissent and allegiance to report back to our Chef. The Busser was perpetually walking to clean up the messes our Chef didn't have the time to address. The Spouse was the person who guarded our Chef's heart. And I was quickly becoming our Chef's voice—earnest in tone, excited to share the details of a course, and always ready with a witty remark. Our Chef couldn't be in every place at once, but as parts of a body we could.

CHAPTER 6
ALLEGIANCE REQUIRES DEDICATION

As anyone in the service industry can attest, there's a lot more to accomplish during a shift than you probably realize—especially when it comes to side work. During an average service, we walk between 10-12 miles (according to the Expeditor's FitBit), lift 50 lb tables dozens of times a day, and are seated for approximately 15 minutes during an average 12-hour service. Doing these tasks on a daily basis was as grueling as some of my most challenging times in the military and brought me to the brink of exhaustion on a weekly basis. Doing these tasks with exacting precision (being verbally chastised if anything was centimeters off) and rapidly interchanging necessary tasks within mere moments, particularly during service, required the absolute capacity of my mental focus. Doing these tasks in a performatively "good" mood with "positive" energy without exception during service needled my emotional stability beyond its boundaries on several occasions. So, it's important to keep in mind that the author has been an academic for the past decade—not a CrossFit trainer or religious guru.

Every restaurant is different, but the following checklist details our daily routine for the front of the house designed by our GM and scheduled with the expectation that any task can, and should be, accomplished in less than five minutes like a train arriving on time at every station. Initialing the checklist meant you took responsibility for executing the item, and if something went wrong during service the checklist was summoned by our Chef to identify the accountable party.

12:45pm
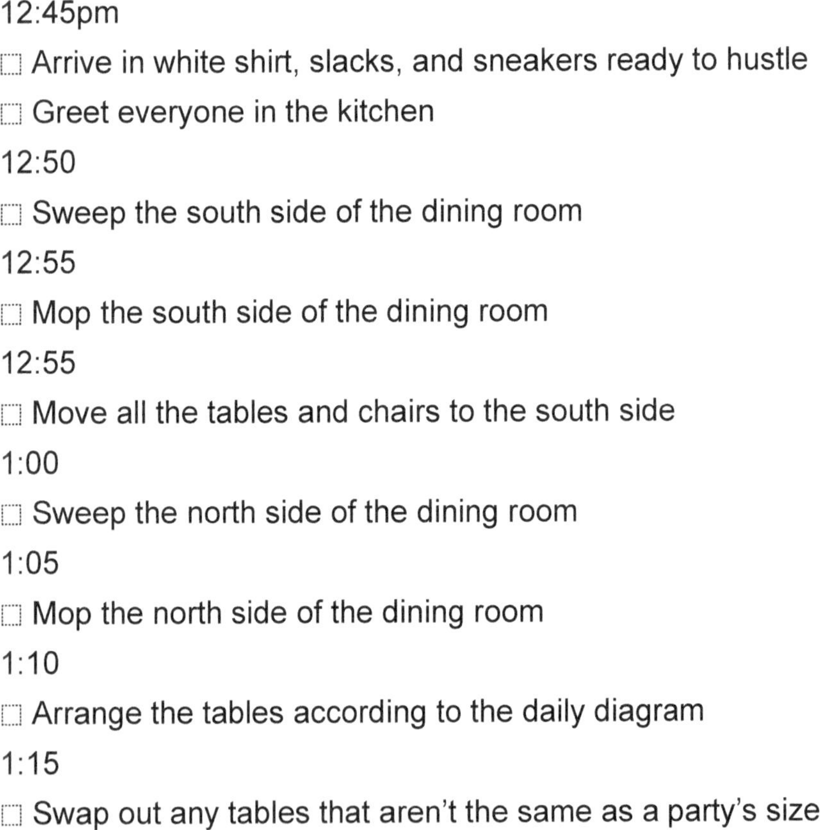
☐ Arrive in white shirt, slacks, and sneakers ready to hustle
☐ Greet everyone in the kitchen
12:50
☐ Sweep the south side of the dining room
12:55
☐ Mop the south side of the dining room
12:55
☐ Move all the tables and chairs to the south side
1:00
☐ Sweep the north side of the dining room
1:05
☐ Mop the north side of the dining room
1:10
☐ Arrange the tables according to the daily diagram
1:15
☐ Swap out any tables that aren't the same as a party's size

1:20

☐ Clean all the tabletops

1:25

☐ Level and balance the tables

1:30

☐ Set all chairs symmetrically around the tables

1:35

☐ Fold, roll, and set the dining room napkins

   (one inch from the table's edge)

1:40

☐ Polish and set the silver

   (centered and one inch from the right of the napkins)

1:45

☐ Polish and set bread and butter (b&b) plates

   (centered and one inch from the left of the napkins)

1:50

☐ Set the dining room glassware

   (aligned one inch above the silver)

1:55

☐ Polish, fuel, and set dining room candles

   (centered six inches from the table's opposite edge)

2:00

☐ Sweep the bar area

2:05

☐ Mop the bar area

2:10

☐ Arrange the bar tables according to the daily diagram

2:15

☐ Clean the bar top and set the bar mats

2:20

☐ Fill the three-compartment sinks in the bar

☐ Fill the espresso machine

☐ Stock the sweeteners

☐ Inventory and stock beverages

2:25

☐ Set bar napkins

   (align with the edge of the bar)

☐ Set bar glassware

   (align diagonally one inch from the right of the napkins)

2:30

☐ Polish, fuel, and set bar candles

   (centered one inch from the edge of the bar)

2:35

☐ Set all flowers in the dining room and bar

   (opinions on their placement will shift throughout the day)

2:40

☐ Blow off and hose down the patio

2:45

☐ Unlock the patio furniture

☐ Swap out any tables that aren't the same as a party's size

2:45

☐ Arrange the patio furniture according to the daily diagram

2:50

☐ Stage the silver, glassware, and b&bs for the patio

2:55

☐ Level and balance the patio furniture

3:00

☐ Fuel and stage the Bunsen burners used for the infusion
course

3:05

☐ Sweep the hallway and private dining room

3:10

☐ Mop the hallway and private dining room

3:15

☐ Clean the private dining room and align the chairs

3:20

☐ Remove the trash from the bathroom

☐ Move bathroom furniture into the hallway

3:25

☐ Bleach and scrub the toilets and sinks

3:30

☐ Dust and polish all surfaces

3:35

☐ Restock bathroom and fold toilet paper into a triangle

3:40

☐ Sweep and mop the bathrooms

3:45

☐ Fold as much linen as possible while the bathroom dries
  (cocktail folds take five seconds per napkin)
  (bar folds take 15 seconds per napkin)
  (dining room folds take 25 seconds per napkin)

(imperfections in the linen are sent back to the cleaners)

3:50

☐ Move furniture back into the bathroom

3:55

☐ Stage all silverware, napkins, plates, and serving utensils

☐ Walk all family meal items from the kitchen to the table

☐ Round everyone up to eat

4:00

☐ Sit down for family meal

4:15

☐ Clean up all items from family meal

4:20

☐ Get dressed for service

4:25

☐ Update any social media assignments

4:30

☐ Everyone gathers for the daily meeting

4:35

☐ Notes from last night are reviewed

4:40

☐ Seating diagrams are reviewed

4:45

☐ Guest alerts (allergies/preferences) are reviewed

4:50

☐ Details of the menu are reviewed

4:55

☐ Descriptions of courses are scripted, memorized, and
   rehearsed for approximately 20 courses

5:00

☐ Print checklists for the patio, tours, bar, and dining room

5:05

☐ Highlight all alerts and menu supplements

5:10

☐ Stock and stage bottles for beverage pairings

5:15

☐ Set and stage all glassware for beverage pairings

5:20

☐ Cut flowers and herbs from the garden for centerpieces

5:25

☐ Set centerpieces in the dining room
   (one inch from dining room candles)

☐ Set envelopes for special occasions in the dining room

5:30

☐ Help the kitchen prep and plate

5:45

☐ Set the lights, music, and light candles for guest arrival

5:50

☐ Fetch ice for the bar

☐ Prepare mise en place for the night's opening cocktail

5:55

☐ Double-check everything including our appearance

☐ Ensure there's a pen, menu, and notes in your pocket

☐ Ensure there's a wine key, table stabilizers, Chapstick, and lighter in your pant pockets

☐ Maybe get a drink of water

6:00

☐ Guests begin to arrive *(detailed in Chapter 7)*

~9:30

☐ Guests begin to depart

☐ Standby until the last guest leaves and departs

X:00

(the time it takes for the last guest to leave widely varies)

☐ Blow out, gather, and store all candles

☐ Gather and store all flowers in the walk-in fridge

X:05

☐ Clean the dining room and bar tables

X:10

☐ Move all dining room tables and chairs to the north side

X:15

☐ Flip all bar stools up and clean the bar mats

X:20

☐ Melt down the ice in the bar and clean the sinks

X:25

☐ Polish glassware until each glass looks like it's new

Y:00

(polishing can take from an hour to several hours depending on the number of beverage pairings, people on staff, special events, and remaining energy level)

☐ Finish polishing and stage the glass racks outside

Y:05

☐ Move all the patio furniture to the west side

Y:15

☐ Lock the furniture and gather all staged items

Y:20

☐ Clean the private dining room table and flip all chairs up

Y:25

☐ Sweep all rooms

Y:30

☐ Pour argon gas in bottles to save the remaining wine

Y:35

☐ Double-check everything is locked

Y:40

☐ Maybe use the bathroom

Y:45

☐ Turn off the lights

Y:50

☐ Drive home

Y:55

☐ Have something small to eat

Z:00

☐ Try to stop thinking about how service went and sleep

○ ○ ○

While most restaurants might not have such a detailed checklist to complete on a break-neck schedule, I hope this gives anyone who hasn't worked in the service industry an idea of what those who work in restaurants for their career, especially in fine dining establishments, have been doing their entire adult lives.

93

CHAPTER 7
DEDICATION REQUIRES PERFORMANCE

Service at a fine dining establishment requires just as much preparation as mounting a theatrical production. Substitute polishing every detail of a dining room with the efforts of a stage crew, rehearsal of each aspect of a course's preparation with a cast of actors running their lines, and you start to see parallels of what it takes to perform an evening's culinary experience.

Daily meetings, much like a script read-through, serve as an opportunity to rehearse and adjust a preceding performance. Our Chef, much like a live production's director, gives notes to the staff and holds everyone accountable for the roles they play (Host, GM, Spouse, Busser, and Expeditor) in executing his vision of the ideal culinary experience. Appearance, expression, and delivery much like costuming, make-up, and elocution are all part of communicating our dedication to diners before guests ever take a bite.

The following script was adapted from my personal notes after dinner service on Saturday, 18 May 2019—one of the most flawless services of my tenure. Of note, it was the fifteenth anniversary of the restaurant and marked my sixth month in service. Of the seven tables served on this particular evening, I performed the majority of the script for each party with the degree of consistency commensurate with the theatrical productions that I've performed in as an actor. Similarly, our Chef, Spouse, and GM all performed portions of the script. The main differences that I would like to point out between a fine dining experience and a theatrical production are that we perform the script for every table and the details of the script at this particular restaurant changed every week, necessitating constant revision.

OUR SCRIPT

Two Guests approach the entrance of a restaurant and are greeted by our Host.

Host: Good evening. Thank you for joining us tonight. May I ask the last name of your party?

The Host marks the reservations list and hands two cocktails to the Guests.

H: Happy Birthday! Here to help start your celebration we have a passion fruit cocktail crafted by our culinary team featuring Hiro Sake from Hiroshima as well as a splash of orange juice and garnished with passion fruit seeds. Cheers.

I understand that one of you has a nut allergy and does not consume seafood. Is that correct? Thank you for clarifying. Our Chef has made the appropriate substitutions and we will ensure that none of those items are plated for you. Now, I understand that it's your first time dining with us. Is that correct? Excellent! We're honored you've chosen to celebrate your birthday with us. We like to treat dining at our restaurant like you're coming to our home for a dinner party, so much like you would at a friend's home, we like to greet our guests with a cocktail and offer a tour of the restaurant. Would you like to join me on a tour?

The Guests follow the Host into a garden in front of the restaurant.

H: I would love to show you the garden first. As you may not know, our Chef decided to consolidate his four restaurants three years ago so he could truly showcase his ability in the kitchen instead of being stuck in metro traffic. Every year we try and evolve our concept to be the best it can possibly be, and we're proud you've joined us for what we currently consider to be the finest culinary experience we have crafted in our 15 years: a 20-course tasting menu designed to be not only the best of what's in season, but what's in season this week. What most diners don't realize is that we source a significant portion of our ingredients from this small garden as well as our Chef's urban farm across the street that his wife tends. For example, you're dining with us at an especially opportune moment when we have strawberries in our raised beds, so for anyone interested I'm happy to pick you a strawberry or you can feel free to enjoy one that catches your eye.

The Host finds two strawberries for the Guests.

H: Everything is organic, so you're welcome to dispose of the stem back in the garden.

You'll notice that we also have a variety of edible flowers such as bachelor's button, diansyth, and nasturtium growing at the moment that will be used as garnish for several courses this evening as well as flowering thyme, lavender, chives, and mint—which is featured in your first official bite of the evening.

The Host lifts a bell jar from a stand in the garden and passes a tray to the Guests.

H: Waiting for us in the garden is a savory cheesecake bite made from sugar snap peas, piment d'Espelette, croutons, lemon olive oil, and mint from our raised beds. Please feel free to take a spoon and enjoy it in one bite. I'm happy to collect your spoons on this tray.

I'm glad you enjoyed it. Now, if you wouldn't mind following me, I would be delighted to show you our bar area inside where you'll be enjoying several more courses later in the evening.

The Guests follow the Host into the bar area inside the restaurant.

H: As you'll notice, we have an exquisitely curated selection of spirits since our Chef likes to highlight particularly unique products from across the globe as well as some of our favorite beverages in the state. As it happens, my father and I are the house brewers and the restaurant features two of our beers at the moment. We're proud to be featured alongside several offerings from two nationally-recognized breweries we've become friends with as well as a world champion meadery and sake maker from a few hours north. During our time in the bar a little later, we'll be focusing on modern takes on traditional bar fare, so to give you a sneak preview, our Chef has prepared your next course to be enjoyed on our tour.

The Host picks up two small dishes and passes them to the Guests.

H: This is a bite of marinated Spanish octopus that's been glazed in kimchi, topped with fried capers, and intended to be consumed like a kabob with a mascarpone-stuffed Castelvetrano olive beneath. Because one of you does not enjoy seafood, we've substituted a watermelon radish for the octopus.

The Host collects the dishes and sets them behind the bar.

H: Thank you for saying so. Now, if you would like to follow me around the corner, I would be happy to give you a peek at tonight's menu in the dining room where you'll be seated for the second half of the meal.

The Guests follow the Host into the dining room of the restaurant.

H: As you can see, our Chef likes to keep things a bit vague so you're still surprised throughout the evening, but rest assured that we will provide everyone with a printed menu at the end of the evening with all of the details to savor.

The Guests read the menu written on a chalkboard.

H: Ah, it looks like our Chef has your next course ready for you in the kitchen. If you'll just follow me, I would love to introduce you.

The Guests follow the Host into the open kitchen of the restaurant.

H: Good evening, Chef. Our guests are celebrating a birthday with us for the first time.

The Chef shakes the guest's hands and motions to two dishes on the counter.

Chef: Thank you so much for joining us. As you might have noticed, we don't like you to go too far without a bite, and I know it's been maybe a minute-and-a-half since your last course, but we're excited to have you celebrating with us. For your next course, we've cured chum salmon roe in house to create a bite of caviar for you resting on the Chinese spoon. It's taken nearly a decade for me to figure out how to cure the roe in the way they serve it in Japan, so if you don't like it please don't tell me. I recommend consuming it in one bite for the burst of flavor and then taking a sip of arugula vichyssoise from the teacup, which is essentially a leek and potato soup that we've made our own by adding local arugula for spice.

The Host collects the dishes and takes them through a door to the dish washing station.

C: I hope you're not just saying that, but thank you. It means a lot that you've chosen to celebrate with us this evening. If there's anything we can possibly do to improve your experience, please don't hesitate to ask or bring it to the attention of our staff. It's been a pleasure meeting you.

H: Thank you, Chef. Now, if you all would like to follow me back to the terrace, we'll have your next course out to you momentarily along with your first beverage pairing of the evening.

The Guests follow the Host to their table on the outdoor terrace of the restaurant as the Host collects two glasses from the host station and sets them on the guest's table as the Spouse approaches.

Spouse: To help you celebrate this evening, our first beverage pairing is a 100% blanc de blanc non-vintage Champagne from Larmandier-Bernier in France. They call their Champagne "Longitude" because all of the grapes are harvested from Chardonnay vineyards along the same longitude in the region. Cheers.

The Spouse leaves and the Busser places two hot hand towels on the table and pours water moments before the Host returns with two new dishes.

H: For our final course on the terrace, we have some Pakistani mulberries that come to us locally from Holiday Farms along with a brandy foie gras mousse that we suggest dipping the mulberries in before biting and pulling the stem out to enjoy.

The Host leaves for a few minutes before the Busser collects the dishes and the Host returns with a tray.

H: I'm glad you enjoyed them. Are you at a moment where you would like to join us in the bar area for your next few courses? Wonderful. I'll be happy to carry your glasses for you if you'll just follow me.

The Guests follow the Host to the bar area inside the restaurant.

H: Here to greet you at the bar, we have some chicharrons, or pork rinds, that our Chef has shaved black Périgord truffles over the top of as well as crumbles of house made truffle powder.

The Host leaves as the Spouse returns.

S: Here we have a 2017 Pinot Gris from the Sonoma County winery Jolie-Laide. You may notice that the label is uniquely decorative and that's because the winery collaborates with a creative collective in their community who works with disabled children as a form of therapy. We love their wine nearly as much as their cause and hope you enjoy it with your next course.

After a few moments, the Busser collects the dishes and the Host returns with two new dishes.

H: This course features spot prawns that come to us from southern California that we've turned into a ceviche with tomatillos, pink and white grapefruit, diced avocado, sliced Fresno chili, and a taro root chip on top for some crunch. Because one of you does not enjoy seafood, we've substituted daikon with the same preparation.

The Host leaves momentarily and returns with two beer glasses he sets down and begins to pour into.

H: As I mentioned before, we have our own beer on tap that my father and I actually brew test batches of on premises. We were both in the Air Force and when we finished our service my father used his G.I. Bill to go to brewing school and I used mine to go to graduate school for Film Studies, so when I'm not in the restaurant I'm a part-time professor. We like to name all of our beers after movies and this is a cream ale we like to call "Pulp Affliction". We usually infuse the beer with fresh citrus zest through a filtration housing each night, but tonight we've infused it with red bell peppers to compliment your next course.

After a few moments, the Busser collects the dishes and the Host returns with two new dishes.

H: For your next course, to honor being in the Southwest, we've created what might be the world's smallest street taco. Inside the flour tortilla, you'll find a canelle of ratatouille we've created from locally sourced peppers, eggplant, and tomatoes paired with a spicy rouille sauce, and topped with crumbles of Valencé goat cheese.

After a few moments, the Busser collects the dishes and the Host returns with two new dishes.

H: Up next, we have our take on a fritter made with asparagus and a Japanese condiment called Yuzu Kosho that provides a tangy flavor to the batter that we've glazed with yuzu juice and topped with crispy Oli salami from Italy.

The Host leaves as the GM approaches.

GM: How is everything this evening?
I'm delighted you're enjoying yourselves. For your next beverage pairing, we have a 2017 Old Vine Zinfandel from Bedrock Winery on the central coast of California. It's

very fruit-forward and full-bodied to pair with the elk this evening.

After a few moments, the Busser collects the dishes and the Host returns with two new dishes.

H: For your final course in the bar, we have elk shoulder that comes to us from New Zealand which we've braised in red wine, melted Comté cheese over the top of along with caramelized onions and horseradish between house made Parker House roll to create our take on a slider.

The Host leaves for a few minutes before the Busser collects the dishes and the Host returns with a tray.

H: Are you at a juncture where you would like to progress into the dining room? Fantastic! Please just follow me and I'll be happy to carry the beverages you're still enjoying.

The Host collects the glasses and the Guests follow the Host to the dining room of the restaurant.

H: Here to greet you in the dining room we have a trio of tartares with house made herb lavash and crème fraiche. Our Chef suggests beginning with the sashimi-grade ocean trout that comes to us from Scotland, advancing to the golden beets that come to us locally from McClendon farms, and finishing with the buffalo loin which comes to us from New York. The crème fraiche is intended to be enjoyed between bites. As a substitute for the ocean trout, we've also prepared a Granny Smith apple tartar.

The Host leaves and the GM approaches with two additional dishes.

GM: I see that one of you has ordered our special caviar to celebrate the occasion. Our Chef's selection of caviar comes to us from a fisherman in Uruguay who did a one-time harvest from the Caspian Sea in order to create a sustainable farm for Osetra, or medium-sized, Beluga. These pearls of caviar represent 7/10ths of a percentage of this year's harvest that are considered Gold in standard. Our Chef suggests enjoying the caviar on a non-reactive pearl spoon first by pressing the caviar to the roof of your mouth before progressing to bites with house made toast points, sour cream, and a shot of Russian vodka. Nostrovia.

The Host leaves as the Busser sets two more glasses on the table and the Spouse returns.

S: For your next beverage pairing, we have a 2017 Chateau de Trinquevedel Rosé that comes to us from

France. It's crafted with a blend of Grenache, Cinsault, Clairette, and Tavel grapes to achieve a near perfect flavor.

The Spouse leaves and moments later the Busser briefly returns to collect the dishes as the Host approaches with two new dishes.

H: For your next course, we have a chilled tomato soup made from local heirloom tomatoes that have been refined into a clear liquid along with clusters of Alaskan red king crab, wasabi, pickled red onion, diced cucumber, and dots of basil oil.

After a few moments, the Busser collects the dishes and the Host returns with two new dishes.

H: I'm glad you enjoyed it. Here to cleanse your palate we have an intermezzo of rhubarb juice that we've carbonated to create a soda.

The Host leaves as the Busser sets two more glasses on the table and the Spouse returns.

S: As we transition into your final savory courses, we have a 2017 Domaine Charles Audoin Bourgogne Rouge that comes to us from Burgundy. It's one of our Chef's favorite wines and we hope you enjoy it just as much.

The Spouse leaves and moments later the Busser briefly returns to collect the dishes as the Host approaches with two new dishes.

H: For your next course, we're showcasing morels that come to us from the Pacific Northwest atop a black garlic brioche that we've just toasted for you, smothered in a spring onion cream sauce, and garnished with chive blossoms from our garden.

After a few moments, the Busser collects the dishes and the Host returns with a tray brimming with new dishes.

H: For your final savory course, we have Berkshire pork that comes to us from Washington State. It's been grazing on hazelnuts it's entire life and has an incredible flavor that our chef has prepared in three different ways for you to experience.

The Host sets two dishes down.

H: First, we suggest sampling the tenderloin that has been sous vide with butter, garlic, and rosemary before charring moments ago to pair with a slice of bacon, braised cabbage, and apple cider vinegar.

The Host sets two more dishes down.

H: Next, we suggest advancing to the belly that has been braised with dashi and paired with ponzu, daikon, baby carrots, and cilantro.

The Host sets two more dishes down.

H: Finally, we suggest finishing with the cheek that has been smoked all afternoon on oak chips and paired with great white northern beans that have been cooked with butterfly pea flowers to take on an earthy flavor and violet hue.

The Host leaves momentarily and the GM approaches with an additional dish.

GM: To help celebrate your birthday, our chef has prepared a complimentary sample of wagyu beef that comes to us from Hokkaido. This is the cap of the tenderloin and based on the marbling is grade A5-12, or the highest possible rating of Japanese beef. What makes this protein so sought after is because it comes from a genetic line passed on in male cattle whose fat melts at body temperature, so it literally melts in your mouth.

After a few moments, the Busser collects the dishes and the Host returns with a siphon pot and small Bunsen burner that's lit tableside.

H: I imagine you're reaching a point where you're quite full, so I'm happy to brew you an herbal infusion to help settle your stomach.

The Host takes the herbs and flowers from the centerpiece from the table and places them into the top of the siphon pot.

H: Once the lower chamber reaches a boiling point the water will pressurize into the top chamber to infuse your centerpiece of flowering thyme, rosemary, and lavender from our gardens along with Lisbon lemon, Hawaiian turmeric, ginger, coriander, fennel, anise, and dried hibiscus to create an infusion that will give you a second wind as we transition into your dessert courses.

The Host leaves as the GM sets two more glasses on the table before the Spouse approaches.

S: Here to pair with your dessert courses we have a non-vintage Moscato d'Asti from Cascinetta Vietti in Italy. The sweet notes and frizzante offer a preview of additional delights to come.

The Spouse leaves and the Busser turns the Bunsen burner off as the Host returns with two new dishes.

H: For your first dessert course this evening, we have a combination of strawberries, mango, and baby pickled peaches. The larger strawberry comes to us from Blue Sky Farms, the smaller are Alpine strawberries that come to us from Holiday Farms, and the green sphere is actually a baby Japanese pickled peach that hasn't had an opportunity to grow a pit yet, so you can consume the entire peach. Using the same ingredients, our culinary team pureed each fruit and dripped the juice into liquid nitrogen to create frozen pearls for you to enjoy with zero crystallization, so they melt in your mouth.

The Host pours the infusion from the siphon pot.

H: Also, please keep in mind that your digestif was boiling moments ago, so it's only intended to be sipped once you're ready.

The Host leaves and returns moments later with the Busser holding a small metal cauldron. The Host reaches in the cauldron and places a deflated balloon on the table that quickly begins to re-inflate.

H: Using the same liquid nitrogen that we used to create the frozen pearls, we shrank a balloon for you, and if you'll notice as it re-inflates it shares our wishes of a "Happy Birthday" (written on the balloon) for you.

After a few moments, the Busser collects the dishes and the Host returns with two new dishes along with a container of bubbling liquid nitrogen.

H: For our final course this evening, we're finishing quite sweetly. This is a white chocolate and vanilla semifreddo we've created by essentially freezing a mousse and topping it with ancho chili caramel sauce as well as spiced pecans for one of you. The centerpiece is not meant for consumption, but we were excited when we discovered that we could pour negative 321-degree liquid nitrogen into vanilla spice water to create a fog that takes on the flavor of the water to echo the notes in your dessert as well as cool the table.

The Host pours the liquid nitrogen into the centerpiece and a fog envelopes the table.

H: Thank you so much for choosing to dine with us.

After a few moments, the Busser collects the remaining dishes and the GM approaches with two cordial glasses.

GM: As a nightcap, we would be delighted to pour you a sample of our house made pineapple-cello. Starting with grain alcohol, we infuse this spirit with pineapple for over a month in the same way that is traditionally done with limoncello. We hope it serves as a fitting exclamation point on your celebration.

The Host returns with a gift bag and the evening's bill.

H: As promised, we've included a copy of tonight's menu along with some small parting gifts from us including some beverage coasters as well as baby tomatoes from our garden. Please remember that gratuity is already included in the check.

The Guests place payment in a leather sleeve.

H: May I?

The Host leaves to process payment and quickly returns with the receipt.

H: We hope you have a delightful evening and that we see you again in the not-to-distant future.

The Guests sign their bill and exit with their gift bag.

GM: Thank you so much for joining us. We hope you have a wonderful rest of your evening.

CHAPTER 8
PERFORMANCE REQUIRES COMMITMENT

During the grueling six months it took to craft and polish our script of an ideal evening at the restaurant, I was also teaching full-time at a university two hours away which entailed commuting to a hotel on Sunday evenings in order to deliver lectures to students Monday through Wednesday before returning to my second full-time job delivering plates to diners. I committed to a one-year contract with my university long before our Chef offered me the opportunity in the restaurant and honoring the agreement taxed me at a rate far beyond what I was actually earning. To be fully transparent, I made $45,000 a year for teaching before taxes, transportation costs, food expenses, supplies and lodging. In turn, the venture I hoped would develop into a promotion to a long-term role actually ended up costing me more, in every sense of the word, than I was ever compensated for.

My marriage suffered because I was never at home, and when I was all I wanted to do was rest. My husband expected me to accompany him to church on Sundays (my only day off) followed by socializing at brunch with his friends, but food had always been my closest idea of religion and working at the restaurant was more than enough spiritual reverence for my soul. Moreover, listening to my husband and his friends asking obnoxious questions and placing persnickety orders embarrassed me to no end as I silently apologized through my expressions to our waiters. I felt sorry for them, but even more for myself. The last thing I wanted to do was talk about my week with someone who didn't understand what I was putting myself through to ensure my husband maintained a level of comfort I was slowly realizing might never happen for me. He wanted attention, but I *needed* security.

Back in Flagstaff, as the semester concluded, the director of the college summoned me into a meeting to congratulate me on finishing the year as the "top-rated" professor in the department based on student evaluation metrics, but there unfortunately wouldn't be an award or even the possibility of promotion beyond my current position. They offered me a contract for another year and told me that positions like the one they occupied would no longer be filled after their long overdue departure. The university, like the majority of institutions in our country, was shifting toward a model that preferred to compensate "Adjunct" Faculty and Lecturers on annual contracts like myself at a rate less than a third of what they were making "supervising" our performance in the classroom. In fact, I asked the director at least half a dozen times over the course of the academic year to evaluate the introductory class I was teaching in person to a maximum capacity of 85 students (who were actually showing up) every Monday and Wednesday morning at 8am, but the director didn't want to "come in that early". Nor did *anyone* see fit to evaluate any of the nine courses I taught the entire year.

I was driving from two hours away and living in a hotel room to teach that class (and many others) all while working in an insanely demanding restaurant. One can imagine why I didn't exactly see eye-to-eye with my supervisor from their vantage point high atop the ivory tower where, instead of actually teaching students, they were making $150,000 per year counting the days until their sizable pension fund supported their retirement. The writing was clearly written on the wall that my time teaching would be over for the foreseeable future. I honored my commitment to the university and decided it was time to return my focus closer to home.

By the time I reached six months in the restaurant, short of becoming an authority on wine, I achieved the goals I set out to perform in the first year. Our Chef and the GM knew I turned down the offer to continue at my university, so when the restaurant closed for two weeks during the summer I took it as an opportunity to propose to them what it would take to keep me employed by the restaurant long-term: in short, a 20% raise and a portion of the tips we generated. In response, they took a break to consider my offer, and when we returned they invited me to the wine room to have a "conversation".

According to our Chef, there were three types of conversations: 1) What just happened? 2) What needs to happen *now!* and 3) What will *never* happen. At the time, I had no idea what type of conversation we were about to have, but our Chef's shifting body language indicated a rare manifestation of discomfort. Our Chef started, "You know we're like brothers, so this is a meeting I've been thinking a lot about. I don't normally have to think about things for a long time, but it's seriously been something I've been struggling with the entire break. We all know how important you are here, but I just don't see you as happy as the rest of us are. We *love* it here. There's nothing else in the world we would rather do than run this restaurant. There's nothing else we *can* do, or we'll go crazy. We're in this for life…" But, as the GM summarily finished our Chef's sentence, "You're interested in dating—and we're looking for marriage." Our Chef nodded solemnly in agreement and the conversation (I later realized was of the third type) was essentially over.

Whether it was a question of the expense of keeping me on with the raise I needed to completely distance myself from teaching was beyond the budget, or truly recognizing that working in the restaurant was something I wasn't committed to for the rest of my life, I understood the reasoning. In turn, we agreed to start looking for a suitable replacement for my responsibilities and they would "try their best" to help me find a role in hospitality that could earnestly fulfill the calling I had yet to find. I would finish my commitment to work until New Year's Eve, and then it was time to move forward—hopefully in a more satisfying direction.

119

CHAPTER 9
COMMITMENT REQUIRES TRUST

Once the academic year was over and the decision was made to find someone to replace me, the anxiety of learning to be a cut-rate sommelier in addition to my other responsibilities washed away and enabled me to fully focus on refining my abilities on the floor during service. I was no longer training. I was committed to executing our Chef's vision: achieving the impossibility of a "perfect night". We all were.

Dining with us during this period was like being in the presence of an orchestra conducted to maximize every note of a timeless composition. Our Chef's focus on precision required exacting adjustments to the menu every day down to a fraction of an ounce or decimal of a degree like a conductor raising their baton an extra centimeter. Our Chef de Cuisine's ability to prep and plate dozens of intricate courses for dozens of discerning guests demanded the technical mastery of someone playing an entire percussion section by themselves. Our GM's attention to ensuring every crumb was cleared and each purse was met with a tuffet was as delicate as a violin soloist. Our Expeditor led the woodwinds, our Busser provided the brass, and I sang my heart out. Our show was sold out every night and tickets were impossible to get.

However, achieving our level of performance on a nightly basis required more than commitment. Pushing the boundaries of perfection drove us to obsessive extremes. What most people would view as textbook signs of mental illness such as obsessively counting everything, compulsively aligning dishes symmetrically, and uncontrollable outbursts of hostility were hallmarks of everyone's conduct when we weren't on the stage. Whether our shared behaviors as a group were conditioned or a cocktail of our combined genetics put us at odds, the resulting environment was as toxic as a rock band about to break up by most professional standards.

Being trained to spot the slightest trace of dust on a table, smear on a window, or hair on the floor like Shao Lin monks with superhuman vision from their kung-fu training in a 70's film meant the restaurant was described by the Health Department as the "cleanest restaurant in the Southwest". Yet, it also meant that it was difficult for anyone in the restaurant not to compulsively clean our own homes like we were on prescription drugs, resist the urge to clean public restrooms whenever we went out to dinner, or spend family gatherings distracted by how much *better* items could be polished and arranged. Being chastised for failure to use the last inch of a carrot, wasting an ounce of cream, or mistaking taro root for daikon meant produce in our restaurant was respected with the reverence of Indigenous hunters. Yet, it also meant that it was difficult to turn those expectations "off" at home and in public.

After all, we could all do "more" to clean our surroundings, take care of ourselves, and eat healthier—all the things we do at the restaurant, but fail to do at home. As a result of my training, it's nearly impossible for me not to sample what I'm working on in the kitchen, make improvements to seasoning that I can still hear our Chef dictating, and enlist the help of squeeze bottles, a mandolin, and Microplane to help plate a night's dinner. It's extremely difficult to separate the value of knowledge for the discipline it took to learn.

Malcolm Gladwell has infamously noted that it generally takes 10,000 hours to master a skill. So, besides early onset arthritis, what do you get when you polish over 10,000 wine glasses? You gain the ability to spot the tiniest of chips around the brim of a glass, immediately identify whether hard water has left any marks, and smell from several feet away whether it's been thoroughly cleaned. It's like having the lamest of superpowers that might as well be a curse. Turning "restaurant mode" off is difficult. There's simply no comparison to other lines of work I've encountered—particularly in the academic community. For those like our Chef, some have the ability to shift their professional demeanor as soon as they cross the threshold into the kitchen and forget any potentially personal slights they may have dished out during service by the next day, but I could never delineate between the two.

By the time I'd made it to my halfway point at the restaurant, my counselor had already referred me to a psychiatrist to help calm the overwhelming mental racing and anxiety I was experiencing. I exhibited signs of PTSD. Although my body pleaded for rest from the notoriously long shifts, I couldn't stop thinking about mistakes I'd noticed, insulting remarks guests made, or potential ideas for improving our service. It wasn't uncommon, when I did get a few hours' rest, for me to sleepwalk to areas of my house and my husband would find me muttering about how a course was "dying at the pass" and "desserts need to walk right now!" There were countless nights when I'd return home and eat cold leftovers over a trash can because I didn't have the energy to use the microwave or dirty a plate. There were many nights I drank far more than I should have in order to forget the day and pass out rather than continuing to ruminate. And there were even more evenings when I returned home to my husband confrontationally awaiting my return like I'd been cheating with the restaurant.

The emotional, physical, and mental exhaustion felt like being in the military all over again. Folding napkins in precise fashion at work turned into folding underwear at home for a room inspection. Washing surfaces within an inch of their lives at the restaurant turned into cleaning tiles in my bathroom with a toothbrush. Carrying martinis across a crowded dining room without spilling turned into ensuring my dog's water bowl didn't spill as I walked across my living room. Knowing the six minutes it took for a sink to fill and figuring out that I could make three trips to the ice maker to fill the trough before returning to the sink to stop the water turned into timing my ability to fetch the newspaper outside, go to the bathroom, and take out the trash in the amount of time it took a pot of coffee to brew.

As someone diagnosed with manic, obsessive, and borderline traits that I now take medication to help steady, working in a restaurant was possibly the worst professional choice for my mental health. Pushing the boundaries of excellence in any field comes at the sacrifice of comfort, but I don't know that it requires the oft portrayed atmosphere in popular media of hostility in celebrity kitchens. Perfection has a cost and everyone involved in its pursuit pays. There are millions of people working in restaurants around the world, and I think they'd all agree that there are better ways of handling the pressure from supervisors as well as guests than resorting to anger or substance abuse.

It's vital to realize that positions in restaurants rarely come with benefits. I was incredibly fortunate to use my teaching benefits before I left, but retaining them at personal cost afterward wasn't viable for my wage. Paying out of pocket for medical treatment, of whatever variety, is something that few people in the industry can afford. As I witnessed with members of our staff refusing to be seen for anything from severe burns to persistent colds that simply needed antibiotics, we all needed more help than we were willing to take. During this period, a fellow Chef and friend from another restaurant passed away due to alcohol poisoning from his addiction, and it's a tragic loss I'll never forget.

The toll the service industry takes on those like my friend who commit to stay in it *for life* is unmistakable. When our GM eventually found my replacement, I immediately saw the trademark signs of submissive conditioning in the philosophy they recommended to me that, "I needed to separate the personal from the professional and not take things so seriously," and the way their hands shook from rationalized alcoholism. They were calloused for the journey of a lifetime, and I was far too sensitive to endure for the same length of time.

Our Chef was always careful not to have anything to drink during the day or on a "school night" and I have no doubt that those self-imposed rules had grown from the persistent reminders of how many brilliant and hardworking members of the culinary community he had been near who's passing was never given the public acknowledgement provided to celebrities. I knew that I wasn't the only one suffering in silence—we all were in some way—but at least we could trust everyone in our family to look out for one another. At least that's what I believed at the time.

Many go through long periods, if not entire careers, as anonymous ghosts in the service industry. So, while my struggles with coping in the restaurant and wrestling with the strain it placed on my marriage pale in comparison to many, the experience taught me an invaluable lesson in empathy: we could all use a little more help.

CHAPTER 10
TRUST REQUIRES HONESTY

Private events were unusual at the restaurant because of the performative style of service and extravagant expense, but during my final week there were two: a holiday party for a national company's executive staff and a 50th birthday celebration for one of our regular guests. The former pushed our physical capacity of 24 guests to its very limits with 30 people in attendance. The latter finally broke my spirit and caused me to sever my professional relationship with the restaurant.

When I started, the capacity of the restaurant was set at 20 guests (or nine tables) by our Chef. However, as the year began to draw to a close, a sense of urgency to try and make the year more profitable was palpable. There was never an announcement, but once October arrived the guest count began to creep up to 24 guests and be "overbooked" on a nightly basis. It may not seem like much but growing by 20% in the dining room meant sacrificing details of service that physically couldn't be met compared to the level of attention given to 20 guests. 24 will never be 20.

Four more people meant a larger profit margin for the restaurant, but nothing additional in the form of compensation for the staff. Extra effort was not only expected, but commanded, by our Chef to, "Work 20% faster!" So, after two grueling months of operating beyond our usual capacity, which was already considered "insane" by our colleagues in the service industry, hemorrhaging our guest count to 30 people for a private party was like having dinner at a drive-through hamburger joint while awaiting a heart transplant. Nevertheless, our new capacity was 24 guests unless you had enough money to make our Chef an offer he couldn't refuse: 30 guests times $200 plus 8.6% sales tax, 22% gratuity, and an open bar meant a gross revenue of at least $12,000 for the evening. Most local restaurants struggle to reach that number in a week, so turning down the event was never even a consideration.

Beyond the difference in scale, private events meant two significant alterations to service: passed hors d'oeuvres on the terrace and larger tables to accommodate 8-12 guests per table in the dining room. Of course, walking trays around clusters of guests at the onset of service was a welcome substitute for synchronized service on the patio with tours, but it also carried the promise of humiliating condescension from guests who were there to socialize among the elite stratosphere of society who could afford to attend such an event rather than appreciate the world-class culinary experience we prided ourselves on. The amount of waste from private events was always shameful. Half of the hors d'oeuvres were never consumed and the same behavior held true in the dining room.

Precious ingredients like caviar, sea urchin, foie gras, king crab, duck breast, truffles, and elk loin were routinely dumped in the trash unless we snuck bites from untouched trays on our way back to the kitchen or subtly donate untouched plates to the workers in the dish pit. Guests at private events could care less about the intense labor it took to create the culinary confections and polished ambiance in our restaurant. It was something we all took personally, and our Chef always regretted halfway through service. The restaurant needed the money, but it came at the sacrifice of the honor associated with our craft. Private events always created a lose-lose situation.

After being ignored by guests while passing neglected hors d'oeuvres, patiently waiting for drunk guests to pause their raucous conversations to describe dishes that would be mocked for including items they had never tasted and would discount without a single bite, and calling upon every member of the restaurant's staff in order to walk to tables of 12 for the style of exacting synchronized service our Chef expected of us, everyone's mood grew sour from the taste left by private events. By the time guests would finally leave, which was inevitably after additional hours of after dinner drinks and sometimes cigars on the terrace, the entire staff was pushed to a breaking point. From my experience, there was never a private event when our Chef wouldn't take his frustrations out on each member of the staff and dispense barbed criticisms we ruminated on into the wee hours of the morning.

The GM was no different. Anxiety about adjustments to service would manifest themselves in the forms of passive aggression and muttered insults as he engrossed himself in fussing about micro adjustments that needed to be made to place settings. As our Busser would repeat hundreds of times during private events long after the kitchen staff would leave and we polished seemingly endless racks of glassware without a shred of hope for overtime compensation, "It's too much, amigo. Chef only cares about the money. This shit is crazy!" He was right on every level. At the end of this particular evening, the host added a $1,000 tip for our "outstanding service" that would've gone a long way to ease the stress we had all been through, but by policy it all went to the house. The sour taste in our mouths had grown bitter, and it was only a matter of time before we grew angry.

○ ○ ○

My final service was originally scheduled for a double shift on New Year's Eve, but I regrettably couldn't make it that far after service for the second private party we hosted during my last week—an event that literally transformed the entire restaurant including the parking lot into a "circus" in order to celebrate a guest's 50th birthday with 36 of her "closest" friends. As we found out the night before (technically the morning of the event after we finished polishing only hours before), we needed to park several streets over to ensure there was enough room for a big top tent to be erected by the party planner's crew before we arrived an hour earlier than usual. The GM insisted we keep questions to ourselves until the day of the service, so we didn't get "too far ahead." The GM's temper was short, and his eyes kept darting away to avoid our gaze. We all could sense that the circus was going to be a shit show, but only the GM knew the details of just how bad it was going to be. If he told us, we probably wouldn't have showed up.

The morning of the circus, I rolled out of bed only a few hours after our last shift ended, made some coffee, and drove back to the restaurant to find that the transformation was already well underway. A crew of a dozen workers were unloading three overstuffed U-Haul's that were spewing decorations like a pinata. Fake six-foot hedges had been staged to cordon off the restaurant from passersby on the sidewalk like an elegant crime scene. A false ceiling had been installed around the terrace using upside-down yellow umbrellas that hovered above an oversized red carpet. Large spools of fabric had been draped from the ceiling to the floor of the dining room to create the effect of being inside a hot air balloon. And, as promised, the entire parking lot was in the middle of being converted into a dance floor with a DJ booth, space for acrobats to perform on a pole, and a vacant space where my Replacement needed to build a second bar later in the evening while guests were in the dining room. We had lost complete control over the restaurant.

As I made my way into the kitchen to greet everyone, our Chef seemed unusually distracted by the whimsy of it all. "There's going to be a lady wearing a 'living' cocktail dress to greet people with all the glasses resting on her dress. I wish I were going to this party—it's going to be incredible!" Everyone seemed bizarrely upbeat and I genuinely wanted to share our staff's positive mood about how special the event was going to be, but when I started the daily checklist it was immediately clear that all of the tables and chairs had disappeared from the restaurant. "Where is everything?" I asked the GM. He pointed to the trucks and finally started sharing the laundry list of variations we were accommodating for service that evening. The first of which was to work with the assembly crew (who already moved our furniture to an area behind the tent that was exposed to the elements like they were bulk trash) and install the flimsy pop-up tables with plastic chairs they brought. 36 guests meant six tables of six and absolutely zero room to navigate in the dining room when several courses would require six people to walk at a time. Nevertheless, the GM dictated that, "This is what it's going to be!"

The problems only grew worse as the day progressed and the GM quietly barricaded himself in the office. We were wandering around the restaurant aimlessly trying to figure out what was going on and looking for things to do because the vast majority of our routine had been completely thrown out. Meanwhile, the party planner dressed in reflective aviator glasses, fatigue bottoms, and a bedazzled blazer became increasingly more insistent on following his orders like a General staging a coup. Left with few options between escalating to war with the party planner or submitting to his assumed leadership, I gathered our front of house troops and redirected our forces to helping our kitchen staff—who it turned out were deeper in the weeds than soldiers on the ground in Vietnam. Our restaurant was being invaded and it would take everything we could muster to defend our reputation from failure.

For the rest of our time until the daily meeting, the Expeditor helped prep, the Busser plated courses, and I worked in the dish pit for an hour before cooking the entire family meal from garlic roasted chicken and loaded baked potatoes to steamed green beans and a chef's salad. Half of the kitchen's actual family members were conveniently joining us for the meal that day, and of course the party planner had to be fed, so there were at least two dozen people to feed—the size of our normal guest count. As the GM later commented, "We wouldn't have eaten at all today if you didn't help the way you did." Although, while I appreciated his sentiment, there were still a cryptic number of details he was keeping to himself until our final moments before the circus began.

The only time I've written more notes on an alert sheet than my first day at the restaurant was on my last; ironically, a year to date from my first service. It turned out guests would be arriving 30 minutes earlier, we would be setting up a caviar buffet in the bar, cocktails would need to be staged on a performer's dress at the entrance of the restaurant, but their proper arrival would also necessitate not waiting longer than 5 minutes for consumption due to the egg white element of the drink. Moreover, the bar would be open, so guests could call their own orders, we would be walking extremely fragile glassware on glowing light boards between guests during hors d'oeuvres, and nine courses would need to be completed in the first hour of service to keep to the time-table scheduled by the party planner so speeches could be made in the dining room.

The menu was completely different from the night before, so everything needed to be rehearsed and memorized. Plus, the additional nine courses in the dining room would also need to be completed in an hour and a half in order to ensure guests had enough time to enjoy the surprise dance party in the circus tent after dinner. The host hadn't inquired whether anyone had allergies or restrictions, so the plan was to tell guests "We'll see what we can do" if anything was brought to our attention, but as we all knew the answer was always "yes". With 30 minutes left until service after the meeting, the GM knew that we had no acceptable option other than to try and maintain our standards of service as best we could given the circumstances.

When guests arrived, there were cocktails waiting on the "living" cocktail dress. When they made their way into the bar area, there was a kilogram of caviar surrounded by a buffet of condiments for them to enjoy while they ordered their next round of drinks. Guests arrived in Bentleys and Rolls Royce's with the ladies draped in furs and the gentlemen in shimmering topcoats. The extravagant amount of wealth on display, particularly to those of us who were making less than $200 that day, was uncomfortably vulgar. When we weren't whisking cocktails to the entrance, we were checking expensive coats that had been worn for all of ten steps from their escorts. When we weren't checking coats, we were taking drink orders because guests were already arriving drunk and downing their opening cocktail before they even stepped into the restaurant. When we weren't making drinks, we were walking delicately arranged hors d'oeuvres from the kitchen that went virtually ignored by guests who were "already full" or "watching their weight".

The few guests who actually tried the first courses, oblivious to the Busser standing next to me with a tray, would actually discard remnants onto the floor, so when we weren't serving, we were hunched over like flamingos cleaning. The kitchen staff was entrenched in the back, and we were on the front lines trying to advance through machine gun fire. The party's guests were the types of people who get down-right nasty when their whims aren't perfectly accommodated, such as not having Bud Light on hand, so they would instantly demand reparations in the form of attention. The conundrum of trying to consistently provide one of the finest dining experiences in the world while catering to uncompromising demands and personal preferences is a challenge that restaurants have universally yet to solve.

By the time guests began making their way into the dining room for the seated portion of the service, they had already sent all of us, especially the GM, scurrying to the far corners of the restaurant to fetch their fancies. To make matters worse, the ocean of alcohol the guests had consumed had fed into tributaries of wandering speeches as well as lines to the restrooms. There was only an hour and half scheduled for the next nine courses, and the party planner was insistent that the dance party needed to start promptly, so the speeches were painfully stealing time from the kitchen. Food was dying on the pass and our Chef was furious. He couldn't take it out on the guests, so anyone that crossed the threshold to the back of the house knew they would be paying a toll.

Walking courses usually meant waiting for all guests to be present, but things were already out of hand with people up crassly joking with other tables while they waited for the bathroom, so I had to make a judgement call to bypass the GM's standards. We were going to start "pushing" (a common term for immediately walking items) as fast as possible. The Expeditor didn't want to be responsible if the GM or our Chef saw what we were doing, so I took over expediting by assigning the Busser and Expeditor to seat numbers and we all grabbed two plates instead of borrowing three people from the kitchen. "Ready for Table 2. You've got seats five and six, and you've got seats three and four." I nodded my head and we synchronized our service to the first three guests at the table then shifted to the next three. I briefly explained the course as guests routinely continued talking across the table and at peak volume across the dining room with other tables, but we made it work.

Plates were finally moving and the kitchen was lining up the next course—largely in the dark about how we were making it happen, but satisfied that progress was being made. During the remaining hour of service, I barely recall seeing the GM. I noticed him adjusting candle holders and flower arrangements, likely catering to odd requests from guests that the rest of us had started ignoring to focus on expediting dishes. That evening was the first service I felt like the GM had truly been overwhelmed by what undertaking 36 guests in the restaurant actually meant in terms of compromising our—and especially his—standards of service. The circumstances, the guests, and the situation had grown uglier as the night drew to its "epic" conclusion: a tent filled with circus performers and professional dancers.

During service in the dining room, the Replacement I had been training in the preceding weeks had fortunately set up a second bar station in the tent so he could tend to guests' orders while we cleared all of the dishes and broke down all of the furniture inside. Unfortunately, a dessert station also needed to be set up and tended to in the tent where performers were breathing fire and acrobats were contorting themselves on poles. That meant that I was the *only* person left behind to clean up. The GM was processing checks and working with the party planner to set up a parting gift bag station, so I spent the hours that followed trying to process why we weren't getting additional compensation after going through all of the extra effort and enduring the added abuse that private events like the two that week necessitated. I was hired to work a shift—not a circus—so why were the two being conflated?

When I started working that year, after the first three private events I survived during the holiday season, I asked the GM why we weren't getting paid overtime for the extra hours and labor it required to serve private events. "That's our Chef's policy," was the answer he echoed throughout the year, so I knew how he would respond if I asked yet again. It was time to confront our Chef. Unless it was going to be my last night of service, I needed to hear a justification for why I should continue volunteering my service. I needed to at least hear an earnest "thank you" in acknowledgment of going above and beyond already world-class standards or receive a modest request of time-and-a-half for private party shifts moving forward.

Unfortunately, it was too late. The kitchen staff was already leaving. I watched through the front windows of the restaurant as our Chef walked past without saying goodbye while I muttered to myself in the bar polishing racks of glassware alone knowing that there were still two weeks of holidays with my friends and family that I would be missing for the second year in a row. Adhering to our Chef's policy was no longer a matter of personal sacrifice—it was a form of professional abuse we were expected to suffer. The glass I was polishing shattered in my hands at the realization.

That night I came to the conclusion that our Chef didn't see me as someone who committed his life to serving in the restaurant industry; therefore I wasn't worthy of earning the type of wage I needed to pay my mortgage and have the security of knowing that the restaurant would always take care of me like it would for our Chef or the GM. They were looking out for the livelihood of the restaurant, and I could no longer trust them to look after me as well. My abilities had grown far beyond the wage I was earning but would never be equally valued. Emboldened by the decision I made at that moment, before our Chef could cross the street, I leapt from behind the bar and called out for a moment of his time. He stopped and I approached to look him in the eyes with a single question: Can those of us working on shift wages please have overtime or a portion of the tip for tonight's event?

The answer was, "Absolutely not. You're paid by the shift and that was tonight's shift." Disappointment was written all over my face. We were having the third type of conversation all over again, but this time I was on the other side of the decision. I could no longer trust that he would care for me as a member of the restaurant's family, so they could work the rest of the year without me. I turned my back and returned to the bar to clean up the shards of glass on the floor. I finished polishing the rest of the racks and gave my notice when the GM eventually returned. There was no need for further conversation. I was done being a servant.

CHAPTER 11
HONESTY REQUIRES COURAGE

The following service, I turned my keys over and said my farewells to everyone at the restaurant in person. Like every story, for each hardship there had been a lesson, so I hope our Chef would agree that we ended on even terms. I provided a level of insight that helped elevate the restaurant to further heights at a discount in exchange for a year in waiting that pushed me in a direction I may have never taken the time to explore. I was thoroughly humbled by the experience, and it was difficult to leave the team I grew to love and respect beyond words, so I kept my comments simple, "I've learned more in the past year than any other in my life. Thank you all, from the bottom of my heart, for the honor of working beside you."

There were firm handshakes from our Chef and the kitchen, embraces from the front of the house, and even a few selfies with the Expeditor, but not nearly enough time to savor a final bite. I exited through the staff door and took a last look back to wave farewell, but everyone had already returned to their checklists. Looking back wasn't an option at the restaurant, but in the weeks and months that followed I struggled to distance myself from continuing to consider how to make the performance of service even better. My continuance over the past year required increasingly obsessive lengths: ruminating thoughts that fed my insomnia, struggling to recover from the physical fatigue, and dealing with the uncertainty that my future held. I needed time to digest.

The day after I quit, my spouse immediately started planning daily social gatherings to reunite with our collection of friends proclaiming, "I've finally got my husband back!" But the last thing I wanted was to be around people who had never spent a day in service. It felt like returning to regular society after being in the military. I was still processing how I had been changed by the battles we fought on a daily basis at work and no one in our social circle—especially my husband—had a frame of reference for the level of sacrifice it demanded. The discipline the restaurant required sharpened my vision, trained my nose, developed my palette, hardened my body, and bent my spirit to a breaking point. I was initiated to a fraternity of millions who are painfully aware of the disparity that exists between *consumers* and the *consumed* in our culture.

I felt like the service industry spit me out in the same way colleges treated me as a disposable commodity and my husband expected me to abandon the notion of having a career of my own. I had nearly been consumed, and there were days when I felt closer to death than I ever want to revisit. I had completed a *Hero's Journey* to a new world, but wasn't meant to stay at the restaurant—nor was I meant to remain the same in any respect.

Everyone at the restaurant collectively served as my teachers for my year of service, but we all had to accept the truth that my evolution was taking me in a different direction. The call to adventure had come with many sacrifices, but it also sustained me by providing newfound skills and renewed confidence in my ability to endure. My personal growth required severing my professional relationship with our Chef, but I gained the courage it would require to blaze a new path forward in my life on my own terms.

My personal goals for the year were to maintain control of my temper during service, avoid severe injury, and steel myself from shedding any tears. I'm proud to report that my conduct met those goals, although I thought about breaking them on a daily basis. I wanted to see what it takes to survive a year in a world-class restaurant, and I had more than a taste of what it takes to thrive in one:

The stamina of a boxer;

the bandwidth of a computer;

the curiosity of a scholar;

the obsession of a detective;

the bonds of a family;

the drive of a train;

the performance of an actor;

the reverence of a disciple;

the timing of an orchestra;

the submission of a servant;

the spirit of an artist;

and the courage to grow.

CHAPTER 12
COURAGE REQUIRES GROWTH

Nothing changes your perspective as a diner more than working in the industry. From the design of an establishment's signage and the authenticity of a host's welcome to the signing of the bill and a waiter's closing remarks, *everything matters.* On more than one occasion, our Chef recounted to us how at the conclusion of an extraordinary meal at a legendary restaurant in Paris their waiter was nowhere to be found when they were ready to pay. When the waiter eventually returned with the bill everyone noticed that he reeked of cigarette smoke. It was the only thing our Chef can remember from the meal, so we all came to recognize when he cited the memory that there was *never* a moment during service when we could lose our focus if we truly wanted to give our guests the finest experience possible.

There was a reason our Chef inspected the sidewalk prior to guest arrival. There was a reason why we never parked near the entrance of the restaurant. There was a reason we were always ready at least fifteen minutes before service was scheduled to begin. There were thousands of protocols, and for each one—there was a reason. Our Chef, our GM, or someone who suggested an improvement had witnessed something they regarded as *the best they had ever seen*, and that's what we strove to provide on a nightly basis. Cultures of excellence are fueled by a commitment to discipline and an unquenchable thirst for improvement. Operating in such an environment requires extreme passion, so whenever I venture to a new place my eyes are always scanning for signs of *better* and I'm always delighted to unexpectedly encounter it like a dear friend.

My favorite moments of any service were when guests would realize the thoughtful design of *why* we operated in a specific way, set the table in a particular style, and prepare courses using painstaking techniques to optimize the combinations of ingredients. In particular, there were three guests that I always enjoyed waiting on because they acknowledged all of the nuanced flourishes we meticulously scrutinized that would never cross the minds of most restaurants. The diner I admired most was a petite Japanese woman who would come in every month to sample the new menu and dine alone, completely satisfied to savor the experience in silence. It still makes me smile, reflecting on the way she would beam with delight when I would bring a course of precious ingredients to her and describe their preparation with delight. Waiting on her taught me a lot about cherishing the revelatory moments in dining that you'll never forget, so her example is one that guides my own philosophy.

In contrast, my most challenging guests were a couple from New Zealand who would dine with us seasonally and actively criticized us in a constructive way to improve any areas we might overlook. Waiting on them was taxing, and most of the staff preferred to avoid their scrutiny, but I honestly loved it when they came to visit. They had traveled the globe several times over and knew how to play their roles as diners. From their appearance to their demeanor, they understood the dance—the repartee and balance required to facilitate an exquisite meal. An evening with The Kiwi's in the house felt like executing the ideal wedding reception: their expectations were understandably high, but it was always a distinct honor to be entrusted with hosting the occasion.

Similarly, having the former food critic of the Arizona Republic, Howard Seftel, and his wife Kathleen dine with us was one of my beloved evenings of service. I had only met the two briefly at local social engagements, so I didn't know how they might conduct themselves as diners, but I was overwhelmed by how complementary they were of how far we had evolved in their eyes beyond the experience they had previously recognized with *five-stars* and glowing reviews over the course of a decade dining with our Chef. From the tour we guided them on to the act structure of the evening as a performance, they not only noticed—but *celebrated*—every detail. For them to comment that our restaurant had become one of the best in the world made it feel like every day we committed to service that year was a moment rightly invested in our Chef's vision.

Before my year in the business, I thought I was a savvy diner, but there's always more to notice, consider, and learn from. In his book *Front of the House*, which I turned to for guidance in my first few weeks of service, restaurateur Jeff Benjamin dedicates several sections of advice to readers on how to be a more compassionate diner. It's a topic I think about all the time, and something we regularly discussed in the restaurant. What were the most exceptional meals we had enjoyed? What made those experiences memorable? How were other places approaching an ideal diner service? What could we do to make ours one-of-a-kind? In my opinion, it's not only the establishment—it's the guests.

Ultimately, we can set the table and prepare the food, but if a guest projects their anger or entitlement on the staff from the moment they arrive, it's always going to be a struggle instead of a dance. When I made this realization, it helped me grow as a diner and as a person. After all, how would you like to be treated? Whether it's in personal relationships or professional endeavors, one of the overall lessons I took away from this period in my life was acknowledging how much my conduct as a diner was a direct reflection of my character in all aspects of life. As a result, I've changed several characteristics of my behavior as a guest that are intended to serve as closing reflections for anyone open to having a dinner conversation with me.

Arrival

There's a famous line in Brett Easton Ellis & Mary Harron's *American Psycho* when the main character, a sociopathic Wall Street banker, proclaims that he's not going anywhere *without a reservation!* While I'm generally against sociopathic behavior, I've got to agree on this point: It's always better to reserve a table instead of showing up and making demands. When I see a group of six arrive at a restaurant at 8pm on a packed Saturday night and try to intimidate a host to produce a table like a ticket at the gate for a fully booked flight, it makes me want to call them out like correcting an entitled passenger trying to cut their way in front of those of us patiently waiting to board a plane.

Nearly every night of service at our restaurant there would be at least a couple of people, if not a large group, who would wander in during service and expect to be seated, immediately requiring very audible attention that would disrupt our guests. Not only that, but they would demand an explanation for why we couldn't accommodate them on such short notice. "But there's a table right there. Can't you just seat us there and bring us a menu?" Unfortunately, we cannot. However, I can produce a business card from my breast pocket and kindly encourage you to come back on another evening when we have an opportunity to properly prepare. It's not that we don't want you to join us, it's that we don't have extra food prepared, staff available, or even enough dishes to set a table for you. Please make a reservation.

And when you do, please honor it. I can't stress this enough. Never will I ever double-book an evening and at the last minute decide which reservation to honor. It's completely disrespectful to an establishment that not only costs them business but creates waste in an industry where every ingredient is precious. Don't be the flake who RSVPs for a dinner party and doesn't show up. Be a person of your word and if you want to behave with an air of class, we would all appreciate it if you showed up as close to on-time as you can. Arriving an hour late completely ruins the days of painstaking work it takes to orchestrate the perfect evening. Think of a dining experience like having tickets to a show and you'll start to understand why I apply this philosophy to my own scheduling.

Electronics

Smartphones have revolutionized society, so it's only reasonable that dining norms follow suit and develop updated considerations when it comes to etiquette. When I go out to dinner, I like to think about my phone like we're about to take flight—set the internet on airplane mode, silence the ringer, and turn off the sounds for incoming messages, typing clicks, and especially the camera shutter. If you want to take pictures, we consider it a compliment and utterly encourage you, but out of respect to the other diners it becomes incredibly distracting if the shutter noise is activated and you're taking hundreds of pictures to the point when it starts to sound like we're at a fashion show instead of hosting a meal. Having the noises activated on your phone serves as a distraction to yourself more than anyone because it draws your attention away from enjoying the evening and needles you to text at the table at best and answer the phone so everyone can hear your conversation at worst. If I ever need to speak to someone on the phone, my approach is to quietly step outside for a moment. After all, one doesn't have to be a surgeon in order to know how to politely make a call.

Moreover, recent trends such as wearing headphones while dining and even watching movies on tablets during service completely undermine the interpersonal aspects of sharing public spaces. Such conduct comes across as incredibly condescending to workers. Wearing headphones and earbuds while someone is trying to speak with you is a form of disrespect I first encountered in the classroom, but now unfortunately see everywhere—especially when it comes to interacting with cashiers. At some point in American culture, people started attaching headphones to their ears to silence their surroundings, speaking into microphones to hear their own voices, and affixing their eyes to gadgets to avoid making eye contact with others. Common courtesy is sadly becoming antiquated in the physical world as society is increasingly distracted by the digital landscape. I don't think people need to make a singular choice, but I do believe that decency requires making mindful decisions about how we interact with one another—including our devices.

Tipping

A common way of showing appreciation for hospitality services is to leave additional currency for workers, but the act is far more complicated than it seems on the surface. It's important to recognize that every business is different—especially when it comes to distributing tips. My restaurant was unique in the way that 22% gratuity was factored into purchasing a ticket for dinner in advance, but never distributed to us in addition to our wage for a shift. Of particular note, there were two nights I can recall when the hosts left a thousand dollar tip, but the front of the house was never compensated. It was obviously a point of heated disagreement between myself and our Chef that evolved over the course of my year in service. As someone with no previous experience in hospitality, I agreed to the terms our Chef initially presented, but as I grew more experienced and began to have pointed conversations with other workers in the industry it quickly became apparent that the way tipping was structured at our restaurant was exploitative.

To my relief, the week after my departure our Chef finally adjusted his policy to allow the front of the house to accept any tips handed to them in cash. Instead of viewing the change as a personal slight, I saw the gesture as a small professional victory my small act of protest helped secure. Ironically, I'm happy to report that The Kiwis tipped everyone a hundred dollar bill the evening the policy changed at the restaurant's daily meeting, but it isn't just about the extra cash in workers pockets. Tipping is a way of acknowledging that minimum wage simply isn't enough. While creative and empathetic solutions are becoming increasingly practiced in the service industry, there's always going to be a divide between those who *can* afford to dine out and those who *can't* afford not to wait on them.

Growing up in the military, it was common when I was a teenager to bag groceries to earn some extra money beyond an allowance. Depending on the day's volume and one's demeanor, you could make over a hundred dollars in a few hours ensuring eggs were gently packed and engaging in polite conversation as you escorted them to a patron's car. We didn't get a wage, but tipping was generally practiced and paid well enough that the majority of people bagging groceries were actually adults more than twice my age. As a community, the military managed to create an unspoken culture of support for those of us on the other side of a purchase as long as we were willing to provide a service. I'm not sure why the rest of our society seems to expect extraordinary service for free, but I'd gesture that it has something to do with sacrifice.

There's a distinct difference between being *appreciated* and *valued* in an economy. The former is cheap, and the latter is fair. Spend some time making lattes for people placing orders in sunglasses and headphones, mixing drinks behind a bar with two layers of drunks on the other side shouting orders, or interacting with anyone who insists, *"The customer is always right!"* I can guarantee the experience will change your perspective—not only in the service industry, but in every aspect of business. For most workers, choosing the service industry isn't a preference, it's a necessity. So, when I think about whether I want to spend money on an expensive meal where the dishes are valued, I also consider whether the service is equally valued or merely appreciated. Instead of placing a bet on how fairly a business treats its staff, I'd rather use the same money to leave a tip that goes directly to workers.

Restrooms

My third grade English teacher, Mrs. Leong taught me that a person should return anything you use in a better condition than when you received it. It's a lesson that's stuck with me throughout life and holds especially true when it comes to using a restroom in public or at someone's home. If you've spent time in the military scrubbing latrines or maintaining them at a restaurant you know exactly what I mean. People can act like pigs in a sty when it comes to assuming that someone else will clean up after them because *it's their job*, but I sincerely hope after the current viral scare that the average guest will consider leaving restrooms at least in the condition they found them in.

To stress the importance of this point, I want to share one of the most unpleasant and degrading experiences of my time at the restaurant. It involved a family of six with two young teenage girls. Aside from the way the two children were on their phones the entire evening and wasted dozens of courses they neglected, the real distraction was how they kept leaving the table after every course to go to the restroom. It made delivering courses together impossible and even more difficult to maintain the restrooms that they were desecrating with linens strewn all over the floor and trails of water sprayed all over the counter that actually dripped into the dining room.

After half a dozen rounds of this behavior, I thought I had reached the limits of my patience, but the final time I went to clean up after them I noticed that the roll of toilet paper was missing along with the spindle. Did they take it? Long spools of toilet paper had been rolled across the floor, but there was no sign of the spindle. Should I go back to the table and ask? I could feel the stress of needing to move like a ninja to quickly clean the area and return to the dining room, but I couldn't leave it in such a condition for the next guests. With no clear alternative, I turned the restroom upside down like someone looking for their wallet trying to find the spindle. The last place I looked was in the sanitary bin, and there was a large clump of tissue soiled with menstrual blood. Fortunately, there were nitrile gloves in the cleaning cabinet, so I checked the contents of the bin, and low and behold the spindle had been hidden inside the clump of soiled tissue. They had gone too far and I admittedly lost my cool.

I cleaned the restroom in a fury and returned to the dining room to speak with their mother. Within earshot of the young girls, I simply asked, "Ma'am, are you aware of what your children have been doing to our restroom?" The girls went pale white, but only for a moment. They knew what was about to happen. Their mother answered, "No," and immediately took offense: "Isn't it *your job* to clean the restroom?" I replied, "Yes, ma'am, I'll take care of it," and returned to the kitchen to warn our Chef of their potentially being upset by my inquiry. "What happened?" our Chef replied as he looked into the dining room and saw the mother staring in our direction. We both agreed I was done at their table and he told me to wait in the back kitchen to explain the situation. Once he heard the story he was disgusted, but he also knew that he was the only person who could deescalate the situation.

I'm not sure what he said before they departed, but my point in sharing the story is that he never should've had to apologize for the misbehavior of someone's children who should've known better than to treat public spaces as well as people in service like the refuse they pitched onto the floor. In my experience, guests who behave reprehensibly in the restroom by urinating on the floor and doing drugs are the exact same guests who do things like blow their noses into expensive linen and hand their gum to waiters to dispose of instead of politely going to the restroom to do so themselves.

Most establishments don't have the ambitious standard of tending to the restrooms after each guest, but I would guess that the average restaurant has an expectation that they'll at least tidy up the restroom once an hour. If not, things can quickly become unsanitary and necessities might run out of stock. And if they haven't? People like myself and our Chef actually lend a helping hand whenever we're in public spaces. We wipe drenched counters, throw away paper towels that people chuck on the floor, and subtly let staff know when supplies have run out. Not out of habit, but out of respect for the spaces we share. Please leave them at least like you found them.

Attire

One of the conversations I have with students in Public Speaking courses is being considerate of how you dress for an occasion. Your appearance is the first impression you make when you're introduced, so try not to signal to people that you don't care about the audience, location, or the engagement. Granted, the conversation is usually with teenagers in sandals, short shorts, and tank tops, but I think it applies to everyone. Managing expectations and anticipating cultural norms can be tricky waters to navigate, but it's fundamentally about demonstrating a subtle message of respect for the atmosphere that's trying to be created by a restaurant's staff as well as their guests.

As a general rule, try not to be Björk in the swan dress at the Oscars unless you're Björk at the Oscars. For our restaurant, we never communicated a dress code, but virtually everyone would come to dinner in what most would consider "business casual" in American culture—a dress for ladies and at least a button-up shirt with closed-toe shoes for gentlemen. The waitstaff of our restaurant always wore suits with ties, and the kitchen always wore crisp cotton chef's coats buttoned to the collar. Our intention was to communicate to our guests that we want you to see us at our very best. Does that mean we expect you to show up in a ball gown or tuxedo at your very best? Certainly not—unless maybe we're on a cruise ship.

On the other side of the spectrum, we generally expect you not to dress like you're at the gym or emerging from a pornography set. Trust me. I've seen a woman dine with us in yoga shorts and a sports bra for a meal that was over $500 dollars and she was completely oblivious to how much of a distraction it was for everyone the entire evening. That may sound catty, but a woman actually dined with us wearing a gold-colored leotard cat suit to match her cat eyes, so I can attest that she was cattier.

Beverages

Our goal as a waitstaff was always to enthusiastically greet guests at the entrance of the restaurant with a cocktail that we prepared in front of them as we double-checked their reservation in the background and ensured they were seated at the proper table. Our intention was to immediately disarm any hesitance or stress a guest might be carrying with them on the drive. We wanted everyone to feel relieved that they had arrived at our home and we were sincerely excited they were joining us. The strategy wasn't about getting people drunk early in the evening, it was about creating a welcoming atmosphere and imitating the first action a host would usually take at a residential dinner party.

In tandem, within seconds of being seated, guests would have glasses of water to help stay hydrated. Water is incredibly precious in the desert, and I knew it bothered our Chef to have to triple filter local tap water to meet his standards, but water service is a critical aspect of service. I'm not saying every restaurant needs a water sommelier, but it's important for guests to stay hydrated as well as cleanse their palate throughout the evening. For all of these reasons, I personally prefer to purchase sparkling water when I go out to dine. There are individuals (not me) with palates that can sense the discernable differences between Pellegrino and Perrier like Coke and Pepsi, which is why many restaurants have options for guests, but it all boils down to what makes you comfortable and keeps you hydrated.

The same can be said for the vast array of alcoholic options that guests have at this moment in history: Over a hundred beer styles with thousands of producers, wine vintages covering decades and terroir that's produced grapes for centuries, sake from various grains and grades of quality, mead from honey derived from innumerable combinations of flowers and bees, and distilled spirits extracted from or infused with every ingredient imaginable. Chances are you already know what you like, but expecting every restaurant you dine in to have Miller High Life or you won't drink anything is getting a bit too insistent. No restaurant has the storage of a wholesale warehouse, and we want to provide you with the best products we have access to, so sometimes it's worth shying away from your comfort zone to discover something new.

Given the opportunity, we relish introducing guests to unfamiliar beverages that might expand their concept of the flavors that an artisanal beer, cellared wine, or hand-crafted cocktail can impart. Thoughtfully paired with dinner courses, the combination can produce the sublime. Hence, my recommendation for diners (including myself) is to order a beverage pairing upgrade whenever it's offered. The cost might initially seem like buying a car at sticker value, but I can assure you that you're getting more variety throughout the meal that builds toward bolder flavors and actually saves money per glass than you would ordering a la carte. For example, if you're a person who orders multiple rounds of wine by the glass at $15 from a bottle that contains at least 4 glasses, why wouldn't you order a bottle for $40 to get a bit more for significantly less with the demonstration of bottle service to boot? For me, it's an easy choice to make as a generally trusting person, but for the most discerning of guests it's always a pleasure to share a bottle that likely took us having a long-term friendship with a producer or distributor.

There were bottles in our collection that went back decades from incredibly small yields across the planet that were biding their time in our cellar for the right guest to come along and celebrate their attributes, so we always revered an opportunity to open, decant, and pour such rarities. Ultimately, regardless of one's preferences, it's about managing your disposition. If you have three double bourbons before the first course, it's clear to everyone that your intention is to get wasted instead of savoring the evening. I can't tell you the number of people who would get dropped off by a ride sharing service carrying red Solo cups that they would throw into the bushes at worst or hand off to me in exchange for another cocktail when they arrived at best. Such entrances inevitably foreshadow sloppy conclusions. Moreover, excessive drinking, especially distilled spirits early in a meal, can devastate your palate. Want to quickly test if someone was too intoxicated at a meal? Ask them what their favorite courses were. If they say the first two, then I can guarantee that their judgement was clouded.

It's taken the realization that I've been that person at meals as well as dined with hundreds of acquaintances who've been guilty of the same conduct that my own behavior has dramatically changed. Personally, if not indulging in a beverage pairing, I enjoy starting with a pint of beer, progressing to a glass of wine, and finishing with a nightcap of whiskey, but I know my preferences will change as long as I continue to keep an open mind. To each their own.

Clearing

No one wants you to work when you're dining out—especially when it comes to table maintenance. Whether it's dishes, utensils, or stemware, please let the staff clear items from the table when you're finished instead of attempting to hand them off to us in passing. As our GM emphasized on a regular basis, "It's about grace." Believe it or not, we would have involved discussions and practice sessions when it came to the most elegant way to handle table maintenance in order not to disturb a conversation at a table and ensure we were as efficient as possible when collecting items so we wouldn't have to make multiple trips.

Most guests don't realize it, but if you push your items away from you, it signals that you want them gone *immediately*. In turn, that person's area needs to be cleared separately and creates twice the amount of time needed to maintain a table. Much like waiting for everyone to be served to begin eating, it's equally respectful to let everyone finish so the table can elegantly be reset in unison. And if there's a spill or mess of some sort? I imagine that one of us either heard it, or were already watching your table, so it should be attended to immediately. However, a subtle raising of your hand or eye contact with the nearest staff member will ensure that your table is descended on like a special forces team called in to rescue you from an embassy. Snapping your fingers or shouting across the room will have the opposite response. You'll certainly get our attention, but being treated like a pet being trained makes it extremely difficult to maintain our rapport with you for the remainder of the evening.

Of all my dining experiences, the staff at *Central* in Peru performed the most impressive response I've ever seen to a disruption at a table. Admittedly, I spilled a drink during an animated gesture and was horrified. Instead of making a ruckus to draw further attention to our table, however, they actually invited our table on a behind-the-scenes tour of the restaurant while they covertly reset the entire table like it was staged when we originally sat down. They even brought me a fresh replacement drink to boot. *That's world-class service!* Such examples are practices we deeply consider and try to anticipate. While I personally have an industry habit of stacking plates at casual restaurants so a waiter can readily pick them up with one hand, it's an action I no longer take when a restaurant aspires to being elegant. It's far better to sit back and appreciate the technique of timed ballet service from the left and synchronous clearing from the right. Elegance requires precision—and a little room to clear your space.

Patience

A guest should never feel like they're waiting for something. However, it's important to acknowledge that there's a difference between the amount of time it actually takes to craft a mojito and the perception that we're taking our time coaxing the mint leaves to sprout. Time is highly subjective in a restaurant based on one's perspective. For guests, everything seems to take three times longer than it actually requires. For servers, those same five minutes feel like they're taking fifteen, but we're objectively moving at three times the speed the average person would take to complete the same task. Unless you've honestly kept track of the time on your watch, I doubt you've actually waited 15 minutes.

In no other aspect of a restaurant does this apply to more than a completed dish waiting on the pass like a flower wilting in extreme heat. Seconds feel like frantic minutes to the culinary team searching for hands to walk a course to its destination. The pressure is incredibly high to have each component of a course coalesce in a crescendo. When it does, diners notice. When it doesn't, diners *really* notice. And I can guarantee you that leaders like our Chef *always* notice. If a hollandaise sauce broke and needed to be restarted from scratch, requiring less than two minutes, the intensity of the silence for those moments felt like sweating under interrogation lights for half an hour. The days of monastically preparing the ingredients likely took days, so putting their flavor in jeopardy was a cardinal sin.

I can painfully recall an evening when a cold dessert with a mousse was on the menu one week that had to be walked by the Expeditor or Busser within moments of plating as I trailed behind carrying liquid nitrogen in one hand and boiling cinnamon water in the other to create a fog tableside while explaining the course. The timing required that I ladle the boiling water from the hot line (stove top) into a metal cocktail shaker while someone from the culinary team poured the liquid nitrogen into a saucière (gravy boat) for me to pick up. Rushing was always dangerous, and on this particular night I learned the hard way by missing the mark with the ladle, spilling boiling cinnamon water all over my right hand. The mistake immediately blistered and the pain was physically the worst I experienced all year. Instead of making a scene, however, the Sous Chef told me to hold my hand under cold water in the sink while they plated the course a second time. The GM and our Chef weren't available at the moment, so everyone was sizing me up to see if I'd be able to return to finish walking the course. It was a true test of my willpower and strength. So, when the Expeditor asked if I was "good to go," there was no question in my mind whether I was going to return to ladle the boiling water with my left hand this time and explain the dish as if nothing had happened. The burn happened so fast that it left a mark on my hand that drew a border in the shape of my shirt's cuff that visibly divided the blister from flesh.

In American culture, the average diner is used to waiting a little between courses, but our goal was always to exceed those general expectations by never having anyone wait more than five minutes—even if we were injured—before they would have a fresh delectable place in front of them to enjoy. As a waiter, it was incredibly challenging to maintain such a standard, but having a guest comment how much they appreciate our rapid response to their request always made it a bit easier to keep up the pace instead of the unrealistic demands of a society trained by technology to expect instant gratification. Under our uniforms we're just as human as our guests, so showing a little empathy goes a long way. There's likely a reason for any delay you may experience and it's far from intentional. Good things come to those with patience; *eventually* I'm told.

Departure

All evenings must come to an end. How they end, much like an unpredictable final act of a movie or reaching the fulfilling conclusion of a memoir, often dictates how a guest remembers their experience. Did we exceed their expectations or did we falter in some way? We always want to know why in either case. Earning repeat business is certainly part of the equation, but our intention in asking how a guest's evening felt comes from a pronounced calling to refine every service like a knife sharpening with each pass over a stone. Constructive advice is always more productive than receiving superficial criticism. From the invitation to enjoy coffee service or a night cap to the presentation of the bill and the way we earnestly say "Have a wonderful rest of your evening" while holding the door for guests exiting the restaurant, we sincerely hope you remember us fondly.

When I reflect on the services I was a part of at the restaurant, much like the personal and professional relationships my life has known, the periods of struggle have always been overshadowed by the moments of fellowship and celebration—especially at restaurants. A mindset that values growth can overcome any challenge, but it takes courage. A step forward often requires help from the person next to us. Whether it's tending to your mental health, voicing what's gone unsaid to the ones we love out of fear, or honoring the spirit that drives us all to pursue our dreams, knowing how to say farewell with dignity and grace is a hallmark of one's character. Our time together may never reach perfection, but the moments we share will always provide us with an opportunity to experience what it takes to feel better.

EPILOGUE

1 June 2020

Dear Editor,

If you've read this far, please consider this manuscript as evidence of my ability to contribute to your food writing section. They say, "Those who can *do*, and those who can't *teach*," but there are a significant number of us who are capable of both.

Over the past several decades, I've been hired as an "adjunct" professor with little hope of long-term security, but I hope that if you've shared a similar experience and agree that anyone with the discipline it takes to commit their life to the study of a field's discoveries, mastering their practice through first-hand experience, and pursuing their dreams of sharing the knowledge they've accumulated should be celebrated rather than sentenced to living hand-to-mouth.

Although I may lack the amount of journalistic experience other applicants possess, I've lived a life of service in many non-traditional forms: as a child raised by a military community, a student who graduated from an elite academy, an officer who supervised food & lodging operations for our country's soldiers, a speech and debate coach for college students, an award-winning educator for ten years, and a brief period as a host in one of the greatest restaurants in the world. Of all the roles I've accepted in my life, however, I've always returned to writing and been obsessed with culinary experiences.

My former Chef told me many times that, "Everyone should spend a day as a dishwasher in order to appreciate how hard their circumstances can be." I couldn't agree more, whether it be washing dishes in a professional kitchen or teaching the future leaders of industries. Service has taught me many lessons, but none more valuable than empathy for my colleagues and members of our community. People in hospitality are part of a traveling camp who "go when we can no longer stay," but we're all longing for a place of our own.

Many, like myself, are ready to marry into a family instead of continuing to date. We've all been searching for meaningful labor in our lives, and we're through waiting, so I hope you're looking for someone who feels the same way. Together, I believe we can evolve food writing from superficial criticism toward constructive dialogue. All it takes is a little empathy and viewing challenges as an opportunity to grow.

Cheers,
@NickButlerPhD

RECOMMENDATIONS

Front of the House
    Jeff Benjamin, Burgess Lea Press, 2015.

The Restaurants Book: Ethnographies of Where We Eat
    David Beriss & David Sutton (Editors), Berg, 2007.

Le Guide Culinaire (English Translation)
    Auguste Escoffier, Mayflower Books, 1979.

Beyond Mere Sustenance:
    Food as Communication/Communication as Food
    Carlnita P. Greene & Janet M. Cramer, 2011.

Lessons in Service from Charlie Trotter
    Edmund Lawler, 10 Speed Press, 2001.

Honor Thy Consumer
    Savannah Mandel, University of Florida, 2016.

173

A YEAR IN WAITING

A MEMOIR

Nicholas D. Butler

www.ingramcontent.com/pod-product-compliance
Lightning Source LLC
Chambersburg PA
CBHW071420150726
48000CB00001B/413